Heartselling

Heartselling

Alexander Christiani

New York

Heartselling

Cover Design by: Rachel Lopez
Rachel@r2cdesign.com

ISBN 978-1-60037-703-7

Library of Congress Control Number: 2009935984

Morgan James Publishing
1225 Franklin Ave., STE 325
Garden City, NY 11530-1693
Toll Free 800-485-4943
www.MorganJamesPublishing.com

Table of Contents

Preface

The voice came from somewhere toward the back of the room. My eyes darted to the right, searching each row to identify the source of the question. From the stage at the end of the ballroom, I looked over the participants of our three-day program. I gazed into the faces focused upon me. A glaring bank of overhead lights illuminated the front rows from the ceiling, with each successive row becoming fainter, merging into the darkness that extended to walls I could not see. The only light visible across the room was the green glow of the exit signs above the doors.

"Who asked that question?"

Directed by members of the audience pointing to the right, I stepped off the platform and walked to the aisle in the hope of making eye contact. An audience facilitator with a microphone met me at the row where the hands were raised.

"Here I am," a frail voice echoed.

"Good," I said. "I see you now. Would you please repeat your question?"

"Certainly," the tiny voice of an older woman whispered into the microphone. "After being self-employed for thirty-five years, I wonder: Is there a strategy for lasting success in business? And if there is, could you boil it down to its essence—maybe condense it into one or two sentences?"

I heard the question the older businesswoman was asking. I sensed the underlying sincerity as my mind listened to the words. In the circles of my friends and colleagues, success strategies were common topics of our everyday discussions. We discussed the strategies, techniques and applications of business success over long-distance conference calls. In my recollection of these conversations, however, we had never discussed whether lasting business success could be condensed into one singular formula. Not really. This lady was doing her work well. By asking her question, she was inviting me to draw an answer from deep within myself to a question I never had been asked this way.

The audience was silent, hundreds of faces focused on me. It was one of those moments that occurs only rarely. Somehow her question went deeper than the levels of logic and reason. I had little idea of what to say. Trusting the process unfolding between us, I opened my mouth, curiously listening to myself.

"The key to lasting success in business," I began, "is to win the heart of your customer and keep that love relationship alive!"

That was all! My response was complete. A silence fell over the room. Together the audience and I paused to consider the power and simplicity of those twenty-one words. I thought about what I had said. Could it really be that simple?

Isn't the key to a lasting romance winning the heart of your loved one—and then keeping that love alive? Isn't winning the heart of your kid and then keeping that heart-to-heart relationship open the first prerequisite of being a good parent? And doesn't that recipe—winning the heart of your partner and then nurturing the relationship—work with friends, neighbors, and employees alike—whether you want to build a lasting sports team, a company, or a church?

Could it be that all of us intuitively know already: the key to lasting and prospering relationships is winning the other person's heart and then nurturing that relationship!

Why don't we admit this truth when it comes to business?

The question of the old lady, her courage to speak up with her tiny voice in front of several hundred people, most of whom were strangers to her, and drawing that response from me served not only each of us at that moment.

Over the years, that same response has served many people in many cities. And it helped me understand much better what marketing and sales is really about: Do we really want our partner to win us over with

"Guerrilla Marketing Strategies" or do we want him or her to take a course in "Romance Relationship Management" where they learn to present their "Unique Selling Propositions" to us? Do these and other marketing and sales strategies really point the way to winning our customer's heart? Or aren't they—more often than not—disguising?

What would happen if we took the wisdom in our hearts seriously and looked at all marketing and sales approaches from a new paradigm—the perspective that lasting business success depends on winning our customer's heart and keeping that relationship alive?

Pondering over this question for years, I identified seven magnets that powerfully attract the heart of your customer:

1. First Magnet: **Being unique:** Did you ever watch a mother or father describe their newborn baby? Although for most of us, newborn babies look very much alike, for their parents (and grandparents) they look very special from day one. Whether it is their hair or the shape of the baby's tiny fingers or toes, if it is our own, it is special to us and we look for the baby's uniqueness. The same process occurs every other time our heart is touched and we fall in love. Did you ever hear newlyweds proudly exclaim, "I'm so happy. My husband/wife is totally average. I'm so ecstatic—there is absolutely nothing special about him/her"?

That doesn't ring a bell, does it? And there is a reason for that: *To touch our hearts, there has to be something special*—and whether you call the building of this special profile in the business world "positioning," building an "expert status," or "branding" is not important. *Building a profile of uniqueness in an area where it matters to the client is the First Magnet to attract his heart.*

2. Second Magnet: **Being trustworthy**: Trust—as we all know from our personal relationships with spouses, family members and friends—is a necessary prerequisite to giving up layers of protection and allowing others to touch our hearts. The more initial trust we have, the faster the process of relationship-building; the less trust there is, the slower and more stressful the process. The paradox with relationship-building—as we all know—is this: Not knowing

somebody equals not trusting the person. Not trusting equals not allowing him or her to communicate with us in a trust-building way. This leads to the question: What is one of the fastest ways of building trust and making new friends? The answer is: Being introduced by old friends. This is the reason behind all the other reasons why word of mouth is one of the most effective marketing techniques ever discovered. The relationship between a company and a new client already starts with a high trust bonus given by the person who offered the referral—and this is what makes word-of-mouth a very strong magnet to attract the customer's heart.

3. Third Magnet: **Getting in touch and staying in touch**—in a beneficial way: When we look at all the people who got to know their significant other through their work, at the gym, or at any other place that provides lots of opportunities to meet, we don't need to be a rocket scientist to figure out that contact opportunity is essential or at least very helpful in starting relationships that touch the heart. We also know from our personal relationships that the *appropriate contact frequency* is the next natural step in long-term relationship-building. But here is the key point: Although a lot of people meet every day at their workplace and have high contact frequency, only some of them develop meaningful personal relationships. And here again—looking from the perspective of our personal relationships—we all know intuitively about the kind and the quality of contacts that attract the other person's heart: *It happens when our focus is on them instead of on us; it happens when our partner feels valued and appreciated, it happens when we offer them the opportunity to feel better in our presence than they would without us.* So our Third Magnet for attracting the customer's heart is about the quantity and the quality of—to use a term from the business world—our "Contact Management."

4. Fourth Magnet: **Team environment:** If you like being with your friend, but all his other friends are boring to be with, chances are, you won't enjoy your friend's parties too much. If your parents-in-law are boring and everybody they surround themselves with is robbing you of your energy, maybe that puts a toll on your relationship too.

And vice versa: if the family of your wife or husband is one of the most empowering families you've ever met, if spending time with them boosts your energy on a regular basis, you figure out that "being married to somebody meaning being married to their whole family" is really enjoyable. Looking at your business from that perspective, it becomes clear that no matter how attractive your "Starbucks" or "Apple" brand personality may be, *if the team in your store doesn't match the expectations set by the brand, your long-term success is in jeopardy.*

5. Fifth Magnet to attract your customer's heart: **Communication skills**: As much as you may love your spouse, your mom, your dad, or a friend, if the other person is not a good communicator, chances are this deficit will hurt your relationship in the long run. If they are great communicators, you know from experience how much value that adds to your relationships and how attractive and heart-touching that is. The same is true for your sales and service people and everybody else who represents your company. The greater their communication skills, the better their ability to convince the customer, the stronger is your Fifth Magnet in touching your customer's heart and building a lasting client relationship.

6. Sixth Magnet: **Self motivation** or the factor of "radiating eyes": We all are attracted by highly motivated people who radiate energy and are willing to go the extra mile, whatever the task—and we all know how contagious and heartwarming this energy is and how strongly we all feel drawn to these energizers. So what's the main difference between a five-star hotel compared to a four-star hotel? Does the five-star one really always have the bigger pool or the fancier entrance hall? Sometimes yes and sometimes no; the real difference between a world-class hotel and its lower-ranking competitors seems to be *how motivated the employees are to walk the extra mile for their guests.* If the top hotels can use this kind of motivation to attract and keep their customers, you and I can do it too!

7. Seventh Magnet: The last magnet was the hardest to discover. For years, our consulting company used the first six magnets to support our clients in winning the hearts of their customers. And while getting

through the marketing clutter and really focusing on what it is that matters to win the customers' hearts worked well for most of them, we knew that something was missing. Time and again, we had clients who organized their marketing and sales strategies around the concept of heart selling but still didn't have the breakthrough success most of our other clients had. And then one day, it dawned on me. While I was watching a talent show for kids on TV, I witnessed that each kid won the heart of the studio audience instantly; it didn't matter whether their talent was in singing, dancing, or acrobatics. *Observing the beauty of talent in action mesmerizes our hearts*—and finally I understood. There was another factor of attracting customers that we had never addressed before. The receptionist at the five-star hotel who is a real "people person" and radiates his genuine joy in connecting with people, the chiropractor with the mesmerizing golden hands, the world-class speaker who touches us by reminding us of the wisdom we have been carrying in our hearts already—they all displayed great talent. It is no accident that we all enjoy witnessing great talent in action, whether it is in sports, music, art, or business: ***Talent*** *magnetizes our heart in its own way*. This insight finally made way for the consistent breakthrough: only when you make sure that the right people are in the right place, your company's organization will unfold smoothly enough to attract your customers' hearts each and every time.

Whether you are a business owner, a marketing professional, or a sales expert, you know that rarely a week passes by without you and me being introduced to a "brand-new breakthrough" marketing or sales technology: "All there is branding"; "the only thing you ever need is word of mouth"; "Customer Relationship Management"; "One-to-one-Marketing"; "Guerrilla Marketing"; and—yes, I was even offered "Piranha Marketing." It is easy to lose sight of the forest with all these trees in front of you.

Deep inside, we already know the formula for lasting business success: win your customer's heart and keep that love relationship alive. The best way we found to put this insight into action and build your company faster and stronger than you ever thought possible is by using the roadmap of the Seven Magnets. You will find its easy-to-use step-by-step action plan in subsequent chapters. I invite you to become a "heart seller." Whenever you sell from your heart to your customer's heart using the Seven Magnets, you will find yourself on the most elegant and effortless path to lasting business success.

Don't take my word for it—give it a try and see for yourself. You'll be happy that you did!

Alexander Christiani, January 2010

Chapter 1: Heartselling—Discovering the Pulse to Your Customer's Heart

If the rumors are true, I may be able to save my business. If not, I am committing career suicide, using the last of my resources and time. Sipping a macchiato in the charming little town of Starnberg, Germany, on a crisp Monday morning would have been a treat at any other time, but today John was praying for a miracle. *I flew 10,000 miles to meet an internationally known marketing "guru." If he can't help to rescue my company from decline, I may be even faster out of business than I can think ...*

The repetitive, bizarre dreams had started months ago. John had ignored them, considering them irrelevant, until they came into vivid focus. Finally, one day it hit him when he was reading the newspaper; his eyes caught the sub line of on article written by the neurologist Donald Calne: "The essential difference between emotion and reason is that emotion leads to action while reason leads to conclusions." John's inner voice turned up the volume. "This is why the solution to all your business headaches lies in Heartselling!"

John had never even heard the term, but his intuition piqued his curiosity enough to research "Heartselling" on Google. He discovered a German marketing master who had coined that term and was well known for his seven paths to the customer's heart—a system he called the "Seven Magnets."

When John started reading about "Heartselling" through the "Seven Magnets," it all made a lot of sense. The only disturbing factor—John chuckled when he thought of his prejudice—was that this guy was from Germany instead of the United States! The United States continued to hold the spotlight as the fiercest market in the world for sales and marketing. How could anybody anywhere else in the world have figured out something that eluded the brightest American marketing experts?

The more John researched the Heartselling system, the more he was convinced that it must have to do with the power of German engineering. Loving Porsches and BMWs, John had told his wife when he left, "If there is anything in the world that Germans are really good at, it is figuring out powerful systems. Maybe they took our best marketing ideas and put them into one system focusing everything on marketing and sales to address the customer's heart. If Heartselling is about what I think it is, then it may be exactly what the doctor ordered."

Stopping his train of thought, he reminded himself of the reason he was here and waved for the waiter. After paying his bill, he crossed the busy street—tense and excited to see if the Master held the answers he required. It was 10:00 AM exactly when he approached the imposing mansion surrounded by a generous lawn. He rang the bell in anticipation.

The Master himself greeted John at the door. "Welcome. I hope your trip was comfortable. If my experience holds true, the clients that travel the furthest are typically the most committed. Flying 10,000 miles seems to be a great indicator that you are really interested in finding your customer's pulse and learning the secrets of Heartselling."

John looked doubtful as he replied with a frown, "I'm happy to meet you. I am committed. But I'm not so sure about being successful. Keeping my best customers is a constant struggle. The competition is fierce. I know my business. I stay current on what's new and fresh in marketing. But it's confusing. Every expert has a different opinion, and they seem contradictory. One says it's positioning and branding. The next says the key is word of mouth. Yet another says the only important thing is one-to-one marketing and strong customer relationships, and nothing else really matters. Then someone else comes along and says all of that is outdated because buyers are too sophisticated, so all you need is a good sales channel on the Internet." Taking a deep breath, John shrugged. "It gets confusing, not to say discouraging."

With a knowing smile, the Master spoke. His smooth voice gave John the first glimmer of hope. "Come in. We'll get started right away. I am well aware of how confusing it is. I have studied most of the 'gurus' for over twenty years. I'm appreciative of the education I have gleaned from their brilliant ideas … and I am equally appreciative of the blind spots I see in their philosophies. It does not take a rocket scientist to figure out what most marketing and sales approaches are missing. Think about Guerilla Marketing—it's one of the most popular marketing approaches for small and medium-sized companies.

"The interesting question is: do you and I expect to fall in love with a company and build a long-lasting, trustworthy relationship with this company, knowing that it is targeting clients with guerrilla tactics?"

The Master's smile broadened mysteriously. For a moment, John felt as though he was on some adventure to recover an ancient lost secret. The strong German accent quickly brought him back to the present.

"The experts have failed to address why marketing requires more energy and investment," the Master confirmed. "Over the past two decades, however, this has been less effective year after year in developed markets. And the experts won't solve anything until they address the two root causes."

"Okay, you have my attention. What are the root causes?" John's foot was bouncing. He could hardly contain his excitement, a detail that didn't go unnoticed by the Master. John felt the first glimmer of hope forming. Maybe these rigid German engineers had fine-tuned their systems and were actually putting this system into action. BMW and Porsche were beating the hell out of the competition worldwide. Sure, everyone knows of and respects the efficiency of German production processes, but how could they have taken that know-how to develop a system to address the customer's heart and make him or her fall in love with the company?

Without ceremony, the Master began his lesson. "Root Cause number one: for 3,000 years, marketing was successful. About 150 years ago, marketing 'experts' effectuated a paradigm shift that was dead wrong, yet they have refused to change it, even though it is obviously failing."

"Wait a minute," John interrupted. "Are you trying to tell me that the antiquated marketing of our ancestors from 3,000 years ago was successful and that the modern marketing of the past 150 years has been wrong? Furthermore, that the shift made 150 years ago is responsible for the mess we have today?"

"Exactly," the Master replied, "and it's easy to prove; just look it up in the dictionary. The word *marketing* is derived from the Latin root *'mercatus,'* which means 'doing business in marketplaces.' When I first heard that definition, I thought it was redundant. However, as I explored it, the rationale behind the definition began to crystallize.

"Imagine living in Rome 2,800 years ago. As an everyday event, we go to the marketplace. There we find three young 'entrepreneurs' yelling to draw our attention toward their produce. One calls 'young carrots,' the next 'big carrots,' and the third 'cheapest carrots; you can't beat my price.' The beauty of this approach is that we actually appreciate and enjoy the process. It helps us make our decision. We show this first of all by actually going to the market. This system worked because we wanted to be talked to.

"The marketing principle of informing and selling to people whose heart was open to be served because they invited us to do so worked for 3,000 years. Then, on 1 June 1855," the Master paused and smiled. "Ernst Litfaß, a book printer in Berlin, got permission to set up 150 billboards in the shape of pillars. That was the birthday of interruption marketing. On that day, the paradigm shifted away from 3,000 years of focusing on the question: How do we listen and respond to customers and their hearts' desires when they come to us? Instead, entrepreneurs began thinking: *How can we get to the customer? And how can we carry the market to customers who aren't even present?*

"The answers to this question are the reasons for the push marketing, overkill advertising, and the general mess that you are in today. Customers are sick and tired of 3,000 or more "buy me" commands every day. They hate that they cannot get to their airplane without being asked twice whether they want another credit card. They are turned off by advertisers buying the first eight pages of a magazine, because they cannot find the table of contents with the articles they bought the magazine for in the first place.

"With this kind of marketing, it should not be a surprise to anyone that he is losing clients, or that you have to work harder to get them. You should be surprised that you have any at all."

John nodded, a little confused but willing to go along. "All right, if 'How do we get to the customer?' is the wrong question, then what is the right question?"

Pleased with John's enthusiasm, the Master leaned forward, gazing directly into John's eyes. "The paradigm needs to shift from selling psychology to buying psychology. The strategic question is no longer, 'How do we get to the customer?' It has to be, 'How can we invite the customer to buy from us?'

"The most overlooked point by most marketing experts is that people love to buy. They are driven by the need to buy. Psychologists tell us that people have a lust for buying. Consumers love to feel that they have discovered a great deal. Both men and women love to shop. Only the products they are drawn to differ … possibly high-tech toys vs. clothes, but the process is the same. All consumers love to be informed, even seduced when they are interested, and have decided show up at a marketplace. However, they hate having products and services shoved down their throats.

"So the marketing paradigm for the twenty-first century is:

> **How can we draw a prospective customer to us intelligently and invite him respectfully to buy from us? Knowing that reason leads to conclusion and emotion leads to action, we could rephrase that question to: How can we attract the buyer's heart by opening our own heart and touching them? The answer to this question is what the Seven Magnets of attracting customers is about!"**

The Marketing Master smiled at John, adding, "In case you think—like many of my clients—that this approach is common sense and is already used by every marketing expert, do a search on Google for 'sales psychology' and 'buying psychology.' When I did so recently, I found a ratio of twenty sites for sales psychology to one site for buying psychology. Buying psychology is still a very new field."

John was convinced. He wanted to know everything about the "Seven Magnets." But he didn't want to get ahead of himself. "So one of the root causes is that sellers began attempting to push their own preferences instead of responding respectfully to the customer's desire to buy. But didn't you say there were two root causes? What is the second root cause of the mess that marketing is experiencing now?"

Impressed with the clarity of John's mind, the Master continued. "The second root cause is simple." He smiled. "Are you familiar with Edwards W. Deming, the world-famous American quality expert?"

"Yes, I know of him," John replied. "I believe he is the father of the Japanese quality movement that propelled Japan into a dominating position with unmatched standards in multiple industries worldwide."

"Exactly." The Master nodded. "Dr. Deming discovered that 94 percent of the reason that things go wrong, i.e. that projects are not finished and targets are not achieved, is a result of the underlying systems in place, and only 6 percent is a result of the people making mistakes in executing the system.

"This philosophy makes it easy to understand why some of the greatest marketing ideas executed by the experts don't work in your company. The reality is that you don't have 'experts' implementing and integrating these systems into your operations. While these ideas may be great, they are not usually incorporated into an effective system. In addition, most of the gurus who have developed great systems have not had the foresight to relate them to other great marketing ideas.

"According to Dr. Deming, you only influence the marketing results with your actions by about 6 percent. The other 94 percent can and will be delivered only when you incorporate a system that integrates all of the great ideas about marketing and sales into one powerful 'marketing machine.' Therefore, the real question is: **How can all great marketing ideas be integrated into one powerful marketing machine producing the desired results?"**

Smiling confidently, the Master proceeded. "Are you ready?"

John was overwhelmed with excitement. If the system could deliver what the Master promised, he may have found the answer to his marketing challenges. John exclaimed, "It's hard to believe that one system could integrate all of the greatest marketing ideas I've ever heard of, but you hooked me! I can't wait to get started."

The Marketing System of the Seven Magnets

"The beauty of the system of 'Seven Magnets to touch your buyer's heart' lies in its simplicity. It reduces complexity so that a twelve-year-old can manipulate it. Let me give you a brief overview; after that, we'll look closer at each magnet until you have mastered it."

Going to the drawing board in the spacious office, the Master drew a picture, explaining, "The three hearts represent three layers of systems that work for or against each company as it builds a relationship converting prospects into customers, and customers into raving fans."

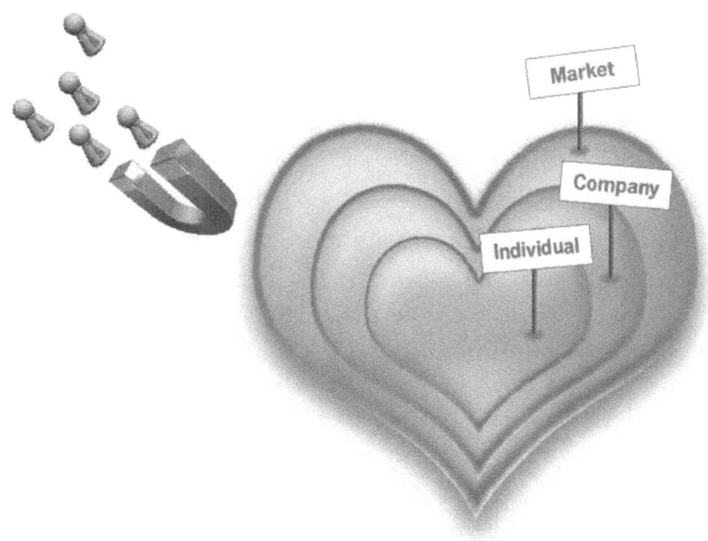

The three-level system of a company attracting customers

"The outside heart represents the market. On this level, the company and its competitors interact with their clients, suppliers, shareholders, and the public. This is the level of the heart that radiates into the marketplace.

"The middle heart represents the company itself, inclusive of the employees and support systems working more or less effectively together to produce the products and services offered.

"The small heart in the center represents the individual that bridges the company and the customer. It could be the sales representative, a service agent, or anyone who interacts with the client in the name of the company—the person who touches the client's heart directly."

The First Heart Magnet: Being unique through expert positioning

Pausing to confirm that his student was following, the Master asked, "John, you appear to be in good shape. Do you participate in any sports?"

"Yes, I'm an enthusiastic tennis player," he reported. "Last year I won the Senior Tennis Championship in Orange County."

"Congratulations!" the Master replied. "Let's imagine next time you prepare for this event, you overdo it and get tennis elbow. Maybe for the first time in your athletic career, you enter the market of orthopedic services." He added, "Now, let's imagine that the three-layered heart of each company consists of seven magnets that might draw you to a specific orthopedist. Do you know who the leading orthopedist is in Orange County for treating tennis elbow?"

John thought for a moment. "No, not really."

"What a huge opportunity for sports orthopedists in your area. It seems that none of them have activated the first powerful magnet in their favor, which is being unique and positioning oneself as an expert in a certain niche."

The First Magnet: brand/expert status

"Let me explain. Whenever I travel to Germany, Austria, or even Switzerland and I ask for a famous orthopedist, more than 80 percent of the respondents say Hans-Wilhelm Müller-Wohlfahrt from Munich. Even if they live 1,000 miles away and would never consider going to Munich for medical treatment, they know this doctor. For more than twenty years, Dr. Müller-Wohlfahrt has been the sports orthopedist of the National German Soccer Team and the personal physician of Boris Becker. A few years ago, Boris pulled his thigh muscle preparing for the Australian Open. He called Dr. Müller-Wohlfahrt to treat him. The next day, every major German newspaper reported that Boris asked his doctor to fly thirty-two hours to Melbourne to treat the injury of probably his most famous patient.

"So the question is: Why do people like to hear about Dr. Müller-Wohlfahrt? Why are they interested in reading his columns in newspapers and magazines? What do Dr. Atkins and Dr. Bob Sears and Dr. Eric Beaverman and Dr. Bob Arnot do differently from dozens of their competitors?"

All of a sudden, the Marketing Master paused, and there was an intense silence. Switching gears, he looked directly into John's eyes. "Do you have kids?" he asked John with a smile and caught his student completely by surprise.

"Yes, I'm a father of two. Daniel, the older one, is eight years old now, and Deborah is six years old," John replied, obviously very proud of his kids.

"Would you agree that your kids are very special to you and your wife?" The Master continued smiling warmly at John.

"Of course they are very special … not only to us but also to their grandparents, their friends, their teachers … basically to everybody they come in contact with, because they are really magnificent kids."

"I bet they started being special from very early on," the Master continued, and his smile broadened. "I could even imagine they started being special to you the minute they arrived in this world."

"This is true. Daniel had really dark skin and was completely bald when he was born. But he had the cutest wide hands like my father and me … it runs in the family," John went on very proudly.

The Master interrupted softly. "Are you aware of his first secret to make you fall in love with him?" he asked.

John was a little confused. "No, not really."

"Did you ever meet a mom or dad who told you, 'My son is completely average. He is exactly like everybody else and that is the reason I love him so much'?"

John shook his head and the Master continued. "There are dozens of books on positioning, branding, and building an expert status—and they all tell you how important those are. And all of them are right. But since none of them knows why they are right, they have a hard time describing the process of expert positioning correctly:

The key to why expert positioning works is that it provides the uniqueness for the customer that allows him to fall in love with the

company. Only if you keep in mind through your branding process that your intention is to create uniqueness to invite your customer to fall in love with you, your positioning process will unfold to be completely successful.

"Whether you call the process of positioning a product, a service, or a person in the mind of the customer branding or simply positioning, as Al Ries and Jack Trout did in 1967, is up to you. What is crucial to understand (and a lot of experts do not) is what this process is about. A brand is not Nike's 'Swoosh' or the three stripes of Adidas … **Successful positioning, being a brand, means owning a piece of the customer's memory—specifically a piece your customer feels invited to fall in love with!**

"John, I can't overemphasize this distinction. A brand is not the logo printed on products or company buildings, regardless how well known they might be. Successful positioning or branding means owning a piece of property in your customer's mind.

"Imagine you live in a town with 50,000 inhabitants. Imagine further that there are three doctors and three Italian restaurants in town. I would bet that one of these three doctors has at least 30 percent more patients than his colleagues, and that one of the Italian restaurants is frequented at a considerably higher rate than the others. Both cases are the result of professionals owning an expert status in the minds of the customers. It's that simple. One of the doctors is likely to have an 'expert' standing with a greater part of the population.

"It's likely that people have to wait longer to be served when visiting the more frequented doctor's office (or the restaurant), and they may even complain. This very fact is also reassurance that he is in demand and worth the wait.

"Imagine that I'm your new neighbor, asking your advice about a furniture store and which pediatrician you recommend. If there is a specific store or doctor that comes immediately to mind, then these professionals own a piece of your mind. The sad yet wonderful truth is that millions of businesses around the world have not succeeded in positioning themselves in the minds of their potential customers. It is sad because Al Reis and Jack Trout told the world four decades ago about the mechanisms of positioning. Every entrepreneur should apply these techniques in his company, to his products, and to the services in their customers' minds."

Looking at John with enthusiasm and a broad smile, the Master said, "The wonderful thing about this truth is that because so few companies have succeeded in positioning themselves, even in today's competitive world, nearly every entrepreneur has the chance to find a niche and position himself successfully as an expert—and when you figure out a way that allows you to be competent and lovable, you will have mastered the tools and the art behind the process.

"A lot of 'experts' will tell you that given today's fierce competition, it is next to impossible to position yourself in the customer's mind. But that is simply not true. I will prove to you that more than 95 percent of all entrepreneurs have no clue how to position themselves successfully as competent and lovable experts. The reason is that from the customer's point of view, an expert is usually in a position diametrically opposed to where the expert believes the it should be: If you learn to define positioning from your customer's perspective, which we will do tomorrow, you will quickly become known as an expert in your area with very little competition—and people will be drawn to you because they can't help liking you. Are you with me so far?" the Master asked.

John nodded with excitement. "Then let's look at the Second Magnet drawing your customers' hearts to you."

The Second Heart Magnet: Trustworthiness through word of mouth

The Second Magnet: Trustworthiness through word of mouth

"Recalling your tennis elbow, you said you don't know of an expert that treats that type of injury in your area. So how would you find a doctor? Would you use the phone book?"

John shook his head. "No, that would be my last choice. I would ask around at the tennis club. Many of my friends have had problems and used the services of orthopedists. I would ask whom they would recommend."

"Okay, let's say a friend tells you, 'I had a severe problem with tennis elbow three years ago. I saw three doctors for over six months with no results. I was so desperate that I thought about giving up tennis. Then the wife of a good friend recommended her physiotherapist from India. I cannot even pronounce his name, but I promise you his hands are golden. He treated me with acupuncture, and three days later, the pain was gone. Two weeks later, I was playing in a tournament. I would definitely recommend him, although he is not a medical doctor."

"Well, with that recommendation, that's a no-brainer. I would be excited to try him out," John said.

"Exactly," the Master chuckled. "It is so interesting that even the multibillion-dollar companies that emerged in the last decade like Google, Amazon, eBay, YouTube, to name only a few, were not built with advertising or other means of classical brand building. They were built by generating trust through word of mouth, which was the first step for us to start liking them. When people first started talking about Amazon (pronouncing it in English which is very different for German ears), some of my friends even had to ask how to spell it because no one had seen it written.

"When I ask an audience of a thousand participants at a marketing congress what the most powerful marketing tool they know of is, how many do you think vote for word of mouth?"

"I'd say 95 percent," John answered confidently.

"You're right. I've had groups that size with literally everyone raising their hands. Every entrepreneur knows that word of mouth is the most powerful marketing support available, *but very few people act on that insight.*"

John thought for a moment. "I wouldn't know what to do about it either. Word of mouth is what happens between my clients when I'm not there. I can sell them a good product or deliver excellent service and pray they don't forget me at the next party. The rest is based on faith."

"Most entrepreneurs think that way. To be successful, you have to understand how dead wrong that belief is. It's true that word of mouth can't be controlled like advertising or direct mail, but it can be initiated and influenced to a high degree. Germans even have a proverb about it: 'What your heart is filled with, your mouth is talking about.' In other words, your customers talk about you to the same extent they have emotions for you." Looking at John intently, the Master said, "You will love Wednesday's lesson. There is proof in social psychology that under certain circumstances, word of mouth may be up to 1,000 times more powerful than any other form of advertising. Yet, few experts know how to engineer and use it. Now you will learn to utilize these methods and discover how simple and how much fun they can be. You start by selecting the right customers. Research shows that the Pareto principle holds true: More than of 80 percent of word of mouth is done by less than 20 percent of your customers. The sooner you identify these 20 percent, the sooner you gain advantage over your competition. This is the beginning of your success."

"I am a believer in the concept of word of mouth. Please, can we discuss it more?" The excitement in John's voice sounded close to desperation.

With a reassuring pat on the shoulder, the Master said, "It will wait until Wednesday. Today we will finish the overview of the other Five Magnets.

"There are many ways for you to find a doctor for your tennis elbow. You may use the Yellow Pages, or you may get the number from an ad you see for a clinic for sports injuries. The point is that none of the information channels will magnetize you until they are believable word of mouth or make you trust in the expert status of the physician.

"Although word of mouth is arguably the most powerful tool in building initial trust with clients-to-be, it is, of course, not the only trust-builder in our toolbox. Keep in mind that using other forms of social proof and powerful guarantees will help you build trust in your brand.

"Now let's look at the next layer of Heart Magnets. While at a lower level, they are on the level of the company itself."

The Third Heart Magnet: Getting-in-touch and keeping-in-touch systems

The Third Magnet: Getting-in-touch and keeping-in-touch systems

"In my opinion, Walt Disney is one of the greatest American entrepreneurs," the Master said. "One of his remarkable insights was noticing that in every company there are only two classes of systems. Disney termed them the 'mechanics' and the 'humanics.'

"Mechanics describes the sum of all physical (mechanical and electrical) systems in a company. When you go home at night, you turn off the lights, lock the door, and go to bed. The parts of your company that are left when you sleep, your employees sleep, and your customers sleep, they are—in Walt Disney's words—the mechanics.

"In Disney's model, the next morning, when your team comes back and puts the mechanical systems in place to serve the customer, your team constitutes the 'humanics' of your company.

"The importance Disney impressed upon his employees was that when the mechanics and humanics of a company are not designed to deliver the company's USP (unique selling proposition) to the customer's door, chances are the USP won't be delivered at all.

"As simple, yet profound, as this insight is, many entrepreneurs still have not embraced it fifty years later. What Disney basically taught was:

1. All the company's systems should be focused on delivering the company's USP to the customer (and they should be designed with that clear intention in mind).

2. As long as it is not engineered into the company's systems, and

3. only exists as an intention (for example, 'we want to deliver five-star service'), chances are slim that this good intention will be delivered to the customer's door.

4. "Take Disney World as an example. One crucial difference attracting families to his park (one of Disney's USPs) was the cleanliness of the place. Mothers especially were attracted by the fact that everything in Disney World was extraordinarily clean. This was a huge advantage for families with small children, because it allowed parents to worry less and enjoy more.

"Here is an example of Disney's mechanics, ensuring that this USP was delivered to his guests in a way that touched their hearts. He started by putting a trash can every fifty yards, colored in a such a way that even less-motivated guests could realize and appreciate that cleanliness that was celebrated and valued at the park (which is the prerequisite that they would start word of mouth about it).

"Disney anticipated that some guests would not put their trash into the can, but next to it instead. To solve that problem, Disney designed the 'humanics,' the team of gardeners and cleaners who would ensure that the waste went where it should be. Because his service team was in charge of Disney World's second USP as well, (which is having fun), he taught them not only specifically when and how to clean, but also how to increase the guests' feeling of having fun. John, have you ever visited Disneyland or Disney World?"

"Oh yes, of course; my kids love it. We go every year," John replied.

"Then you may know from experience that Disney's cleaners are usually dressed up as characters, and when you come closer than three yards, they will start smiling at your kids, then at your wife and you. Since most parents love people who are kind to their children—and in this case also entertaining—you are likely to return the smile. As part of his training to make your day enjoyable, the clown will probably ask if you would like him to take a photo of your family.

"Does this give you an idea of how to install mechanics and humanics in a company to ensure that the company's USPs are delivered through to the client—ideally in a way that touches your customer's heart?" the Master asked.

"It makes a lot of sense," John replied, nodding with understanding.

"Then you are ready for the next surprise. On the company level, the magnets work like the little iron magnets in children's toys. They have two poles, and when they are turned in the wrong direction, they repel customers instead of attracting them. Here is an example of that. Let's say you enter your doctor's office to have your elbow treated. Imagine that their system for tracking appointments is not as efficient as it should be. You say: 'Hi, I'm John. I have a 10:00 AM appointment to see the doctor.'—'Oh, I'm sorry, there must be a mistake. You aren't on the schedule. The doctor is completely booked this week.' 'How can that be? You or a colleague of yours gave that time slot to my wife yesterday on the phone.'—'No, that's not possible. Your wife must have misunderstood something.'

"At that point, all the attraction, build-up by expert status, and word of mouth starts vanishing. Let's look what kind of systems you should have in place when a prospect or client shows up at your door. I call them the getting- and keeping-in-touch systems. From a marketing point of view, you should have four powerful systems in place."

1. The Lead Relationship Management System (LRM-System):

"Think about dating. How many people meet their significant other at work, in the gym, or at any other place they habitually go to? It is still a majority of us, isn't it? And that majority now even includes all the people who practice virtual dating. So we don't have to be rocket scientists to figure out that frequent contacts is tremendously helpful in building relationships. So the question is: if that is so obvious, why do most companies still have close to no focus on building a professional-contacts system?

"Have you ever heard any of the marketing gurus talk about LRM? They will teach all day about CRM—customer relationship management. But most of them have no idea how to set up an effective lead generating system ***that touches the prospect emotionally***. We will talk about that Thursday morning."

The Marketing Master chuckled. "I am amazed that in many industries, there are millions of interested prospects every month Googling key terms like 'health insurance,' 'classic car restoration' or 'better sleep,' looking for solutions to their problems. Very few entrepreneurs are smart enough to filter through these millions of 'information-for-free' shoppers to find the few they could do business with.

"There are two really wonderful aspects about this Internet pipeline of prospects. The first is its cost-effectiveness. Imagine, the cost for an entire year is often less than the cost of one ad or the smallest flyer you could print. The second intriguing aspect is: what is a better place to meet your future wife than the one she is emotionally attracted to in the first place? In case she loves horses, it may not be bad at all to introduce yourself at the stable where she takes riding lessons. So, if somebody searches for yoga classes at 11:00 PM, that could mean he or she is really interested in that topic, does it not? Now imagine that they meet you and your treasure chest of information with everything their heart is looking for. This could be an interesting point to start a relationship, wouldn't you agree?

"But this is only the beginning. The next powerful system you will install is ..."

2. The Stay-in-touch Contact Management System

The Marketing Master spoke soberly. "I'm charging some of the highest consulting fees in Europe. Most of my clients earn my fees back within the first three months. The reason is that nearly all of them have been neglecting their clients and their marketing 'back end.' *Show me your client contact management system, and I will show you how much you lose!* Look at your friendships. Isn't it true that some of your friendships cooled off over the years when you didn't find the time to take care of them?

"And isn't it also true that when a friend of yours functionalized the relationship—imagine he calls you four times a year and every time, he asks you whether you could help him out babysitting—that that takes a toll on the friendship too? So the problem with contact management in a business context is not only that a lot of companies still don't have an effective system in place. The other big mistake is that they only contact their clients when they have another offer to make—instead of applying the wisdom of the old German saying: 'Little presents preserve the friendship.'

"With an effective contact management system in place, many of my clients increase their sales volume by 20 percent within the first three months. Would you like this system in your company?"

Before John could answer, the Marketing Master added, "That's only part of it. There are two more powerful systems to touch your client's heart the right way."

3. The Touching-Their-Heart-Experience Pipeline

"John, do you know about TQM—total quality management?"

"Yes, of course! That's the Japanese *kaizen* concept of quality improvement for the production process in incremental steps over years. Car manufacturers like GM, Ford, and Toyota have used it for at least thirty years." John was proud to finally add some input to the conversation.

"That's exactly right," the Master complimented John. "The industry has known for over thirty-five years how to improve the quality of products through the optimization of the production process. But can you tell me what it is that entrepreneurs have done for the last thirty-five years to systematically increase the quality of service processes to win their customers' hearts? How many three-star hotels are continually working on improving every opportunity of guest contact they have, from wake-up calls to supplying snacks for guests from different time zones at three in the morning? How many doctors and chiropractors do you know who work diligently, year after year, on the quality of the service process delivered to their patients? How many of them do give deep thought to the principle 'Different strokes for different folks' and ask themselves how they can put together a symphony of little touches to their customers' hearts, to make sure that they reach out to each and every one of their customers emotionally? That is our third topic for Thursday. Now, last but not least I will introduce you to what I call the Socrates Approach to marketing."

"Socrates? You aren't referring to the old philosopher from Greece?" John did not disguise the astonishment in his voice. He had no clue what Socrates could have to do with marketing. Maybe the Marketing Master was referring to someone in the industry John hadn't heard of.

4. Socratic Marketing: Installing feedback loops that enable your clients to teach you which products and services to develop next

"Yes, the Greek philosopher, that's the Socrates I'm talking about. Do you remember his main concept? Socrates believed that the truth is inherent to people. He believed that people don't have to be taught the truth; they only need to be reminded of it. The best way to remember the truth, according to Socrates, is by asking questions that allow people to activate the right answers.

"I can't believe how many companies currently spend five- and six-figure budgets on market surveys, instead of getting the information they need from their clients for only a couple hundred dollars per year. Although the Internet and e-mail communication are now mainstream in most industries, many entrepreneurs still do not recognize that they can do complete market research of clients and prospects with a few smart Socratic questions and software tools at a cost of less than thirty dollars per month.

"Do you like the idea of inviting your clients to define exactly what is their heart's desire and what they want from you before you develop it?

"Imagine if the engineers that design VCR remote controls asked us what kind of improvements we would like to see on our panels that currently have up to forty-five buttons. More than 90 percent of the people would most likely respond that they use only four buttons: play, stop, fast forward, and rewind. Some may request a language control function to tape something when they are not home, like: 'Hi, I'm going to the movies tonight. Please tape the new James Bond movie on NBC on 5 January at 8:00 PM.' Imagine the first company to design such a remote. That product would sell like crazy because it would simply be what people want. Do you get the idea?"

"Yes, I do," John answered, "and you claim to be able to do this with software for thirty dollars a month, asking your clients what they really want from you?"

"Exactly, but it's even better than that! You can also do surveys with interested people on the Web. That allows you to discover trends and needs of other target groups who are not yet your clients. You can do all your marketing homework in this manner. I will show you how!"

The Fourth Heart Magnet to attract your customer: Humanics

The Fourth Magnet: humanics

"We defined 'humanics' with Walt Disney's model as the sum total of all social systems in your company," the Master explained. "Your leadership style, management systems, the company's mission statement, your vision, and the values demonstrated by the behavior of your team members on a daily basis, they all build a team that either attracts prospects and customers, or repels them by the atmosphere created when coming into contact. So, how can you invite your employees to grow into a five-star service team with whom your customers fall in love with?" The Master paused before he added, "It took me over twenty years of leadership coaching to figure out that there are two easy but very powerful leadership tools that will help you achieve these results in a very short time. That is our program for Friday, before you leave to explore the Alps for the weekend. When you return Monday, we will discuss the last three magnets," the Marketing Master explained before he walked to the board to draw the following picture:

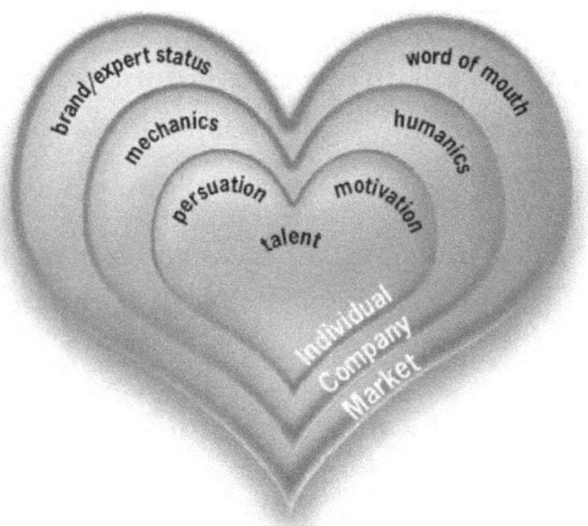

The Fifth to Seventh Magnets: Persuasion, Motivation and Talent

"One of the most important sub-systems of your company when it comes to attracting your customer's heart is the individual who is serving the client and therefore representing you and your company.

We are looking for customer magnets on this level, and actually, we found three of them:

Heart magnets on the level of the individual

"Companies always act through the hands of individuals. As clients, we often notice whether the behavior of the individual working with us is substandard, no matter how great the company is. All the wonderful impressions about the company's expert positioning and excellent word of mouth turn into disappointment. That's why it's critical to attract and magnetize the customer at the level of the individual representing the company. This is the critical point. Here we have found three magnets that really attract customers: communication skills, heartfelt motivation, and a talent for the job.

"All three of these components are simple to comprehend. When you put yourself into the position of a patient in the hospital after an operation, would you prefer to receive a shot from a nurse with 'golden hands' or from a clumsy nurse? Would you prefer a motivated, smiling face greeting you in the morning to a grunting one? Wouldn't you prefer a physician who explains your condition in layman's terms, so that you understand clearly, to a physician who is so technical that he is difficult to understand?

"The component that is less obvious, however, is how to get these three magnets to really work and do justice in your company."

The Fifth Heart Magnet: Communication skills

"Let's look at sales training first. Since the 1950s, sales training and the coaching of service teams have been some of the most popular programs of our soft-skill education in business. So the question is: does the stuff we've been teaching for the last fifty years really work? The unfortunate answer is that when it comes to 'purchasing psychology' (i.e., inviting the customer to buy instead of pushing him), today's sales training is as far from being effective as the ancient Greeks were with their 2,000-year-old tradition of rhetoric skills.

"John, let me share with you my biggest insight in this arena. To finance my studies, I worked as a part-time salesman in the insurance business. I learned all the tricks of closing the deal, but I always felt that something important was missing. Whenever I met a client who was not interested in buying my products—or even worse—had negative prejudices about insurance salespeople, all my persuasion strategies failed. Think of the old rule: 'The one who asks, leads.' This holds true only as long as your partner in conversation has the minimum trust to answer. If that's missing, questions are not helpful at all; they can only make things worse. You know this to be true from discussions with your wife. When you come home and ask your wife, 'Honey, how was your day?' and you get a one-word answer, 'Fine,' you know that something is wrong. The more questions you ask someone who doesn't want to be led by questions, the worse the situation gets.

"Though I felt the persuasion skills I was taught were ineffective when I needed them most, I didn't know where to look for the answer. Then, about fifteen years ago, I attended a seminar in the U.S. with an eccentric coach. The way he started the program was shocking to me. I will never forget it. He ran in, jumped on stage, and yelled at the top of his lungs, 'Heeey, I convince everybody.' He pointed at a young lady and shouted: 'Do you believe your mom was good with you? Let's change that!' He asked her a few bizarre questions like, 'Did your mom always let you stay up as long as it was appropriate, or did she sometimes send you to bed early, only so she could have her peace and quiet?' Sure enough, after two minutes or so, the young lady said, with tears in her eyes, 'You are right, my mom wasn't always good with me.'

"I was absolutely convinced that the demonstration must have been contrived so I challenged the coach. I said, 'Wow, that's really powerful. Can you demonstrate that on me as well?' He asked me to come on stage, asking, 'Where are you from?' I told him, 'I'm from Germany.' He said, 'That's great. Now tell me something that you are absolutely convinced of!'

"'Okay! In Germany we have no speed limits on our highways. I'm a sports car enthusiast. My driving philosophy is *put the pedal to the metal!* So how can you convince me that we need a speed limit?'

"The negotiation master thought for a moment, then said, 'Well, you look very athletic. Do you do any sports other than racing your car?'

"I said, 'Yes, running, working out with weights, mountain biking and skiing!' He said, 'I love skiing too! But I've never skied in Europe. There is a strange thing about American skiers. All day they behave rationally and stay on slopes that match ability. But then, at the end of the day, with tired legs, many skiers decide to try out their superhero powers. They race down steep slopes, very often narrow paths that are icy or rocky.'

"'Same thing in Europe,' I replied. 'At the end of the day, a lot of skiers go for stuff they shouldn't instead of taking the cable car!'

"'Now, let's imagine,' the persuasion master said, 'that you are speeding down such a slope, and in front of you there is a sharp turn with an icy surface. On the ice is a mom with three little kids, all of them beginners, having a hard time controlling their skies. They are skiing toward the edge, with you speeding behind them. What would you do?'

"'No problem; I would slow down and wait until they're all safe on the other side of that ice patch.' He answered, 'I like that. You really consider other people. Now let's imagine another situation: You are on a highway speeding at 100 mph. In front of you is an old SUV going at 50 mph. The driver is an old man who is anxious and upset because he is on the way to the hospital to visit his wife who had surgery that day. He isn't paying attention to his rear view mirror. What do you do?'

"'Well, I call his attention by flashing my lights to let me pass,' I answered spontaneously."

Pausing, the Master looked at John before he continued, "The audience was suddenly very quiet. It dawned on me that my answer was not very astute. If I had any way of knowing about the driver's personal situation, I would be more considerate and patient, the same way I would have been with the mother and children on the slopes. While I wasn't convinced that we needed a speed limit in Germany, I had a profound insight into the benefits of defensive driving.

"All of this was secondary to the actual lesson. The real impression this demonstration made on me was this: seeing my coach accept my challenge and invite me to state one of my convictions before of an audience of 500 people, and admit that according to my own standards, my un-reflected speeding philosophy had some kinks in it. He won me over in less than two minutes. This was a major breakthrough. This coach had some assets of persuasion I had never heard of. During the next break, I ran to him and asked what he had done to my mind. He smiled and replied, **'Human beings can—and often do—refuse to accept what others say. But people are completely open to what they tell themselves. Convincing others of anything is much less powerful than inviting people to convince themselves. All real persuasion is self persuasion through internal dialogue.'"**

Taking a long pause for emphasis, the Master waited for John's reaction. John never looked up. He couldn't write fast enough to keep up with his racing mind.

"To teach your salespeople to invite their clients to convince themselves, start with the process of buying psychology. Monday you will see firsthand how this will boost sales. Now let's look at the next attractor."

The Sixth Heart Magnet: Motivation

"There is great information available on the topic of self-motivation, but our training taught us that most people miss one of the vital points. Tell me, John, on a scale of one to ten, how would you rate yourself on self-motivation?"

John thought for a moment. "Hmmm, not bad, probably a six," he replied. "I'm pretty motivated when it comes to sports, but less so with regard to eating healthy, keeping my desk in order, or cleaning the garage."

"That's exactly what I mean," the Master replied with a nod. "Most people perceive themselves as half or three-quarters motivated. They relate motivation to energy and self-discipline.

"Interestingly, you almost always have the energy to play tennis when you desire, and almost never have the energy to clean your garage. If the true issue were a general lack of energy or discipline, corresponding to your assessment of yourself on the motivation scale, you should lack energy for tennis half the time and for cleaning duties half the time. Clearly, this is not what the evidence shows. We are motivated 100 percent of the time concerning the things we are interested in, in your case tennis. For things we are not interested in, we simply have no motivation at all. You may not have cleaned your garage for months.

"The secret for self-motivation appears to be figuring out which conditions make you feel 100 percent motivated and self-disciplined. When you know that recipe, all you have to do is transfer it from tennis to cleaning your garage and apply it with the same precision. Russian sports psychologists spent years with their world-class athletes researching the specific ingredients for each athlete to achieve their personal best. They discovered fourteen motivation buttons in humans, and every human being has at least three or four buttons that they are highly sensitive to. How valuable would it be for you to be able to teach your employees about their 'hot buttons' and how they can self-activate them to provide five-star service to your clients—starting with genuine smiles and respectful behavior that wins clients over every time they meet them?"

"It would be outstanding!" John exclaimed. "But before I can teach them, I must be able to teach myself concerning the issues I am struggling with."

"Exactly." The Master's smile indicated how pleased he was with John's rapid progress. "That is our program for next Tuesday. Now let's look at the Seventh Magnet."

The Seventh Heart Magnet: Talent

"For years, I have pondered the difference between my clients that struggled to put these marketing concepts into practice while others realized them effortlessly. The obvious difference that eventually became clear was talent. This difference is obvious in sports. The best baseball coach in the world will never win a championship with a second-class team. The difference is not as clear in business. Entrepreneurs often try to coach managers who are not even third class to do a brilliant job. If your sales team needs somebody brilliant to represent you to your best clients and you give the job to an introvert, he may be able to compensate for his shyness to some degree, but at the company party, he'll never be a natural, outgoing, fun-to-be-with party animal.

"There is more to this than matching an employee's talents with his job profile. It may be more important for you, as the employer, to know your own strengths and weaknesses. The myth conveyed by most management books is that a good manager must be good at every job. This is truly a myth. Managers with capabilities in diverse areas—the 'Leonardo da Vincis' of management—are extremely rare. Most successful entrepreneurs and managers have two or three great talents. They are clear about their strengths and weaknesses, and tailor their team-taking accordingly. What they are lacking, they build into a complementary team of employees with strengths to compensate for their own weaknesses. The talent factor is more than attracting clients. It is organizing the talents of your company to effectively execute each marketing task by the person with the strongest talents for the job. Does this make sense?"

John nodded with excitement. The Master said, "Great, that's our program for next Wednesday. On Thursday, you'll be on your way home to put all of your new knowledge into place."

The Marketing Master paused and fixed John's eyes with a smile. "How do you like the program so far? Is it what you had in mind when you were boarding your airplane at LAX?" the Master asked, curious to find out more about John's expectations.

"Honestly, your program sounds too good to be true," John answered with a shy smile, carefully looking for a way to phrase his doubts respectfully. "I'm really fascinated by your approach of Heartselling and the idea that the most important factor for long-term success is to win the customer's heart and to then keep the strong bond of that love relationship alive. And I really love the idea of heart-attracting magnets and your system of describing them on the three levels of the market, the company, and the individual who is serving the client. But honestly, your claims sound unrealistically big."

"Thank you for your open feedback. I really appreciate your honesty. Years ago, when I chose racing cars as a hobby, I had the same feeling when I sat in as a co-pilot with some of the best race car drivers in the world. At the beginning, when my mental map told me that they had to brake or we would miss the next turn, the pros shifted to an even higher gear—and when they finally hit the brakes, I was absolutely sure that we would miss the turn. That happened again and again for the first few dozen laps until finally my map stretched and I learned what a race car is capable of when in the right hands. So what these mentors did for me was support me in extending my mental map to enable me to realize what is possible. That's what I'd like to do for you too—be your marketing mentor and help you stretch your map so you see what is possible in marketing and sales. Does that make any sense?"

John nodded in agreement. "I like that picture. It helps a lot. I think I'm a little overwhelmed now with all the new ideas, and I need a few hours to digest."

"That's exactly what you should go for," the Master agreed. "Maybe you'll enjoy a leisurely stroll on the lake. Looking at the panorama of the Alps usually clears my head in no time at all. One last idea: maybe you want to start writing a diary, put down your expectations and what you have learned over the course of the week."

Chapter 2: The First Heart Magnet—Being Unique: The Secrets behind Expert Status and Positioning

John's excitement woke him before the alarm went off on Tuesday morning. Today the Marketing Master would teach him how to become "pleasantly unique" in the eyes of his customers and position himself as an expert in the market.

The promise was clear in his mind. *Even in the most competitive markets, positioning oneself as an expert is not a challenge, because most experts harbor ideas diametrically opposed to the way things actually should be done. Therefore, there is very little real competition.*

Attempting to keep the skepticism from creeping into his thoughts, John left the beautiful little hotel, Forsthaus. He reminded himself that he had flown to Lake Starnberg for a miracle. He couldn't imagine what it was that every other marketing workshop and qualified instructor had overlooked, but he planned to find out. He would challenge the Master to see if he could deliver on his promise.

The Master opened his home with a warm welcome. John had not yet stepped into the comfortable library before the question escaped from his mouth: "If it's true that most of the experts are positioning themselves diametrically opposed to where they should be, can you give me an example of how to do it right? Why hasn't anyone figured it out and capitalized on it?"

Laughing, the Master patted John on the shoulder. "You are anxious to get started today. It may be very complex if we jump immediately to the punch line. But let's go for it. Last week, I coached a group of 500 pediatricians. I asked what they thought the key to becoming experts in *the minds of their clients* would be. Here are a few of their responses:

- Stay current on findings and research regarding viruses and their mutations to enable them to treat the children in their communities better.
- Attend pediatric conferences twice a year to ensure being up to date on the newest developments in medications and other treatments.
- Post-graduate training in minimally invasive surgical procedures for infants.

"What do you think of these answers? How much impact do you think these strategies will have on making them ***lovably unique*** in the eyes of their clients and therefore positioning them as experts *from a client's point of view?*"

John thought for a moment. "It's impressive. These are all important ways to become better experts in their field, but I don't know whether that would make them lovably unique."

"There you go. Maybe then you won't be as surprised as the doctors I coached. I told them the key to becoming a unique, lovable experts was to have dinner or coffee once a month with a kindergarten teacher."

Shocked, John exclaimed, "You told them to have coffee with a kindergarten teacher to become better pediatricians?"

"Exactly," the Marketing Master said. "That would be one effective way to position themselves as lovably unique in the mind of their clients and patients. You have to admit this is completely different from anything you've heard of."

"That's for sure," John replied. "It makes no sense."

"It may not seem to yet. You wanted it in a nutshell. Voilà, here it is in a nutshell. Years ago, I had a critical insight for successful positioning. My wife and I had just moved to Bad Munstereifel, a little town near Bonn, where we bought our first training center for seminars. Our twin boys were two years old, and my wife was interested in building a support system for them. She introduced herself to our new neighbor, a mother of four children, and asked which pediatrician she would recommend.

"The neighbor felt that having four children made her somewhat of an authority.

'Of course, Dr. Strahl in Rheinbach is absolutely the best!' I became curious to know what it was that made that doctor an expert in her mind. She was adamant. The conversation went something like this:

Neighbor: There are no doctors worth seeing in this town or the surrounding ones. Dr. Strahl is worth driving 20 miles for.

Me: What's so special about Dr. Strahl?

Neighbor: It's hard to put into words, but he *has a heart for children.*

Me: Every pediatrician has a heart for kids. Otherwise he would have chosen a different specialty.

Neighbor: Let me clarify what I mean. When my youngest son was two, he had an allergic reaction to an injection he received. He became very ill and was in pain. It had been a battle to get him to go anywhere near a doctor's office since. When it was time for him to have his required check-up before starting school, he stubbornly refused to go. Dr. Strahl was new in town. A friend recommended him. He was very tall and intimidating when he walked in and introduced himself, especially to a child. But he handled himself differently from most doctors. 'Hi, I'm Michael. Who are you?' My son answered, 'I'm Tobias.' The doctor asked, 'Tobias, do you have the newest Pokémon?' I had no idea what he was talking about. It could have been a disease for all I knew. But Tobias's face lit up. He knew all about the new game the doctor was talking about, as they discussed the different characters he knew from kindergarten. They bonded in less than three minutes. On the drive home, Tobias asked, 'Mom, when will we see Michael again?' I said, 'Are you kidding me? For weeks you refused to see a doctor. I practically had to drag you there. Now you want to go again and get another shot?'—'Not another shot, but when I left, Michael promised to have some new Pokémon characters for me!'

"Now do you see how expert positioning is completely different in the eyes of the client, compared to those of a professional, John? Most pediatricians believe that studying more is the key to becoming better experts. Their clients, however, already assume that they have the professional standard and therefore do not rate this as part of the expert positioning. In the eyes of a mother, building trust with the child is vital, and it ultimately sets the doctor apart from his competitors. It makes him truly unique and is the first step to winning the heart of the parents and their kid. Being able to win a child over the way Dr. Strahl did moved the mother emotionally. She was passionate about telling any mother who was interested in finding a doctor. This is an example of word of mouth demonstrated to perfection."

New light was dawning on John's mind. Expert positioning *from the client's perspective* was very different from what the experts thought it should be. Maybe the experts were missing the trees for the forest. "Isn't it sometimes difficult to discover your clients' needs, even when you are an expert?"

Contemplating, the Master paused before answering. "*The answer depends on whether you perceive yourself as an expert for a specific target group or whether you master a complex set of theories.* As long as you identify yourself as a lawyer, a dentist, a salesperson, a manager, or any specific role, rather than *seeing yourself as a professional with the objective of fulfilling the needs of your customers and clients,* you will eventually disappoint your customers and fail in business.

"Another simple but profound lesson is to stop whining about how difficult things are in business, because they really aren't. If you don't believe me, think about these simple examples:

- It shouldn't take a rocket scientist or millions of dollars for focus groups to discover what mothers are looking for in a family car, yet it took the industry over 100 years to discover that mothers would like built-in car seats that can be easily removed and attached to a stroller with the click of one button.

- It should be a simple concept for dentists treating children to understand that the key component of success in their practice is the ability to bond with children and make the visit fun.

- Why not have a support system for ophthalmology patients or other minor procedure patients? For example, an ophthalmologist I know in Munich told me how he generated leverage to grow his practice. One day he had an eighty-two-year-old patient concerned about surgery. The patient asked if he could bring his ninety-year-old sister, who had had the same surgery, to hold his hand. He became well known among the elderly—through word of mouth—for this progressive yet compassionate approach. Truly a way to win the heart of his patient, wouldn't you agree?"

The Marketing Master smiled at John. "Marketing isn't brain surgery. It took me twenty years to reduce the complexity of positioning and branding to the key elements. You can now master them in six simple yet powerful exercises and enjoy your boat ride on Lake Starnberg, with the panoramic view of the breathtaking Alps by noon."

Positioning Exercise No. 1: The Elevator Test

"John, imagine being in a five-star hotel, having a great day. You are on a business trip. You feel energized and at the top of your game. You are in the elevator. The doors open on the tenth floor. A remarkable, high-profile business executive enters. You recognize immediately that she would be a great asset to your business. She may be the CEO of a major company or the mayor, or some other ideal multiplier for you. Obtaining her business would be the deal of the year. While you are pondering how to start a conversation, she recognizes you and initiates the conversation. 'Aren't you the marketing expert whose newspaper column I enjoy? It's no coincidence that we meet today. I've been thinking of hiring you. But before I do, let me ask one question.' Unable to believe your luck, you say, 'Of course, ask anything you'd like.' She asks, **'What can your company do for me that is unique?'"** The Marketing Master looked at John for emphasis. He said, "Though it may seem simple, don't underestimate the importance of this exercise. If you can't answer this question intelligently, you will have difficulty in business.

"First identify your target group. That defines the desired niche. The stronger your purpose for serving this niche better than the competition, the stronger is your basis to be in business. Start by listing all the promises you would make to your customer to serve her."

Then the Master asked, "Do you want to squeeze everything you can from this exercise?"

John nodded. "I didn't fly 10,000 miles to not learn everything I can."

"When you finish the elevator presentation, underline the promises your competitors would make as well, because by definition, these claims are not unique selling propositions."

John sighed. "There may not be much left on my list if I do that. Most of my competitors are likely to think of the same things to serve the client."

"Claims such as 'excellent service,' 'great quality,' 'customized design,' or 'years of experience' will typically be used by your competition. You don't need to eliminate these from your list. You need to make them believable."

"How do I make them believable if they are not already?"

"It's quite simple. There's a powerful law of persuasion to support you. It states that there are no believability claims made that have no contrary. For example, no one would advertise 'bad quality,' 'late delivery,' or 'choose us, we are unreliable.' So, claiming the contrary is useless.

"Compare a politician whose campaign is built on the premise that he is honest to that of his opponent who promises better support for single mothers. The opposite claims of the first statement leave no alternative, since he would not say, 'Vote for me, I am a liar.' Therefore, his honesty claim is empty. The opposite claims for the second statement have many alternatives … 'Better support for single fathers or support for families,' etc. There is substance and therefore more believability in that statement. Without realizing it, most marketing and advertising claims about quality and service make empty claims that subconsciously are not believable to the customers.

"*The way to make your claims credible is to specify them with facts:* 'Experienced financial advisor' is an empty claim. "Seventeen years of experience, financed over 340 doctors' offices," is a specific statement with appeal for a doctor looking for a finance expert for his office. 'High-quality steel' is an empty promise; 'chrome vanadium steel in the specification surgical instruments are built with' offers much higher credibility."

John was excited. "That's a really powerful tool. I've never heard of it before. I could take the annual report of Enron or any other major company, underline the hollow promises about quality and service made by every other company, and know immediately whether their marketing department was on the ball." He paused for a moment, adding, "It's clear how that will improve my credibility and my positioning as an expert, but I still fear that I don't have any truly unique selling propositions that will intrigue the lady from the elevator and win her heart."

The Master chuckled. He appreciated the way John had of thinking ahead. "Remember, this is the first power exercise of six. The next exercise will address that."

Positioning Exercise No. 2: The Elevator Test in Thirty-six months

"When I was introduced to the elevator exercise many years ago, I was very discouraged. I was a seasoned marketing consultant with over ten years of experience, had a strong reputation, and was one of the ten highest-paid consultants in Germany. However, when I listed what I had to offer, things like 'excellent coaching results in marketing seminars,' I realized that every new consultant would tell their clients the same thing, even if it was misleading.

"It was a revelation to me that with over ten years of shining success, I was incapable of articulating in a convincing way what it was that set me apart from my competition. With some introspective analysis, I learned a valuable lesson: *if I were offered the same chance to do an elevator presentation three years from now, what would I wish to have accomplished in the past three years to sharpen my profile as an expert and brand my company and my products in the mind of my customers?*

"This exercise has proven to be a powerful way for our team to set their objectives at the beginning of each year. It gives a different perspective from sales target numbers and developing new products. It's like looking at our company from the outside. Together we generate many ideas to sharpen our profile with this tool."

Everything the Marketing Master had suggested so far seemed logical and resonated with John, except one. "You mentioned that it's important to develop positioning from the client's perspective. How do I know that my positioning ideas for the next three years are moving in the right direction and I'm not inadvertently making the same mistake the pediatricians made?"

Impressed with his instincts and tendency to remain a step ahead, the Master answered thoughtfully. "The first two exercises will set you up for the right track. They presuppose that you make two important strategic decisions:

1. Be clear about your market, niche, and the target group you are *inviting* to buy from you.
2. Clearly define your unique selling proposition. What is the *unique* combination of products and services only you can offer your target group?

"Once these ideas have crystallized, you can filter them through the next exercise. It will tell you exactly about your chances to win your customer's heart—and it may be one of the most powerful exercises I've ever developed."

Positioning Exercise No. 3: The Bar Stool Test

"While proven to be one of the most powerful, this exercise is one of the most challenging as well. The benefit is that whenever the strategies we developed for our clients passed the bar stool test, the established pattern resulted in success. In ten years, this experiment in thought has not failed us.

"When you have an idea for improving your positioning through the development of a new product or service, it's a good idea to test it with this tool first and continue improving your ideas until they pass.

"Here is how it works and how it was developed. Years ago, I was coaching an orthopedist who managed his private practice himself. When asked how he could provide additional benefits to his clients, he responded with the idea of investing in a computer tomography machine.

"His rationale was that he could improve the quality of his diagnosis with the 3D technology in his office, instead of sending the patients to the hospital, which was then the standard procedure in his field. It was an investment requiring over $2 million, but his clients would have the diagnosis in his office within thirty minutes rather than spending several hours at the hospital. Objectively, I saw the benefit for his clients, but I wasn't convinced that it would have any major influence on his positioning as an expert who wins the hearts of his clients. So I invited him to put it through the bar stool test:

"*'Imagine one of your clients receiving your services today. Later, he is having dinner with friends at the country club. While discussing the day, what's the probability that your service touched your client emotionally or moved him to the point that at the end of the day he continues to think about the value he received, and is motivated to share it with friends over cocktails or dinner?'* What do you think, John? Specifically, what are the chances that a patient who had a CT scan of his knee will discuss how amazing his doctor is because he saved him three hours by not having to go to the hospital?"

"Most clients would not be aware of the alternative. They would take the investment for granted." John understood the point quickly. "But Dr. Strahl, the pediatrician, would pass the test with flying colors. A dentist who shows Disney movies to young patients would also pass. The ophthalmologist who invites his patients to bring friends to hold their hands is another great example of someone who would be the topic of discussion in a bar or at a dinner."

"You understand the concept clearly." The Marketing Master nodded, pleased with his American student. "When you offer something of value to your clients—and that means by definition something that they appreciate emotionally and therefore touches their hearts—chances are, they will discuss it with someone. There is a German saying: ***'What the heart is filled with, the mouth starts talking about.'***"

"I get the idea," John agreed. "Forgive me for sounding pessimistic, but what about industries producing such boring products that it would be out of the question that they could position themselves in a way to be discussed in this manner? For example, one of my brothers constructs and installs production machines for the paper industry. I can't envision anyone sitting around a bar, raving about his toilet paper-producing machines. My sister is a financial advisor. Who sits around the dinner table talking about thirty-year fixed mortgage rates?"

The Marketing Master felt the first hint of disappointment. "Do you know why my clients pay me a small fortune for my personal coaching, even after they are familiar with my ideas about Heartselling and have read my books and attended my lectures?"

"No, I don't." John was curious again.

"As an entrepreneur, you will be successful to the degree that you see chances where less-talented people see problems or nothing at all.

"How many people could have developed a company like YouTube, if they had only seen the possibility that that idea could be successful? By the way, I totally disagree with your statement about boring businesses. Every year I work with dozens of entrepreneurs with businesses similar to your brother's. Over the years, I've seen hundreds of companies. Not one entrepreneur I know believes that the production machines he uses are boring. They are all proud of the quality, speed, environment, friendliness, and overall structure of their best machines. There are no boring industries, only boring marketing people!

"The same is true for your sister's financial services business. In my opinion, there is nothing (except maybe sex) that people are as interested in as money. One of my clients works with the most boring product any financial advisor could offer—basic insurance packages for families. But he promises to demonstrate to families with children how they can save $800 to $1,200 a year on their insurance package. He wraps story after story around these savings. A hundred dollars more every month—you could spend it on piano lessons for your daughter and help her develop her musical talent; you could support your parents with that money, give it to your favorite charity, save it and go on vacation with your spouse. You could invest it in your pension plan for the next thirty years and enjoy a golden retirement.

"We devised an entire communication strategy for him around this benefit. When you log on to his Web site, the savings are the first thing to catch your eye. In his Christmas cards, he asks his clients if they have friends who may not be receiving the benefit savings he provides yet. He has penetrated the market measurably for the last three years by using this strategy. He has over 300 testimonials from families, telling how much money they saved with his program. He gets a tremendous amount of business as a result of word of mouth from satisfied customers who say things like, 'If you want to save $1,000 a year on insurance, talk to our specialist. He helped us so much!'

"I know some of his colleagues who are annoyed with his success. They believe it's unfair that he is mentioned as the expert in helping people save money, even though they are able to do the same for their clients. The industry is full of people who don't understand expert positioning from the client's perspective, even when it's right before their eyes!

"Years ago I coached a friend of mine in Switzerland who is a financial planner like your sister. We brainstormed and came up with an idea that no one else in the industry was offering. He was privileged to have a huge base of wealthy clients in their fifties and sixties. This is the time most people are becoming grandparents. We suggested that the new grandparents give the gift of a pension plan that would make their grandchild 1 million dollars by the time they are sixty-five years old by investing only a fraction of that at the time they were born. The clients were given an impressive certificate in a beautiful frame, on the day of the child's birth, documenting that the new family addition would be a millionaire at age sixty-five.

"With a smart investment fund earning 11.1 percent over sixty-five years, a one-time investment of $1,111.00 by the client, and sixty-five years of compounded interest, the grandchild would be a millionaire by retirement age. That made for an easy selling point. What made this idea even more attractive was that additional certificates of $111.00 could be purchased. This earned the newborn another $100,000.00 for each certificate. So you can never tell me there is a shortage of ideas in the realm of expert positioning, only many people who haven't discovered the obvious yet!"

John's head was ready to burst with excitement. He was finally beginning to understand why the Marketing Master was so sought after and successful in his coaching! He was a genius! In his whole career, John had not come across anyone like the Master, who had obviously analyzed and studied these concepts with a clarity of mind that John had not witnessed in any other expert yet. But John wanted to know more. "What do you suggest for someone who has no clue where to find all these wonderful ideas? Not many people have decades of training to make them locate golden marketing niches where others only see ashes."

"True," the Marketing Master agreed. "If someone has no concept of a bar stool marketing test, I recommend doing the next exercise, the fan survey."

Positioning Exercise No. 4: The Fan Survey

"The fan survey is easy, fun, powerful, and one of the most effective exercises available for building an outrageous service culture. If there is a problem with it, it's that people make it more complicated than it is.

"For the fan survey, determine which of your customers are your greatest fans. This is not to be confused with your largest accounts or the most profitable ones, but rather those who are the most enthusiastic fans of your company. Depending on the size of your company, you may decide to talk to your twenty greatest fans. At maximum, you should choose the most enthusiastic 5 percent of your customers.

"Decide who is doing the survey. Never send an e-mail or letter. Phone communication isn't optimal, except in rare circumstances when you have exceptional rapport with a client. As a standard, the communication should be done in person.

"If you know the client and have a strong relationship with him or her, you should do the survey yourself. If your key account manager or a member of your sales team has the strongest relationship, ask them to do the survey. Either go to their office for the interview or invite your client out for lunch or dinner.

"The interview consists of two simple questions. Depending on the client's answers, there might be a third question for clarification.

1) Mr. Client, imagine a new neighbor moves in next door to you and asks for advice on finding a … (fill in your kind of business here—for example: a good CPA in your area). Would you recommend us to him? Ninety-nine out of a hundred times, your greatest fans will say, "Yes, of course!" (If they don't, you are not asking your greatest fans.) So you ask them the second question:

2) Let's imagine the new neighbor then asks you, 'Why ABC? What is so special about them?' What would you tell him? If your fan doesn't answer with specific incidents or experiences but uses a more abstract description (like ABC really offers good quality), you will ask a third question for clarification:

3) That's great. What would be an example of this (good quality)?

"After dozens of surveys, a common pattern holds true. If you asked twenty of your biggest fans (clients) why they would recommend your company, I would bet on the following:

1. They will describe with some emotion, specific incidents where you went the "extra mile" to help them and touched their hearts.

2. You will have forgotten most of these incidences and will learn a lot about what really reaches your clients, touches them emotionally, and makes them your biggest fans.

3. A pattern will emerge from this collection of emotionally impressive experiences, revealing how your company is already successful at turning clients into loyal fans.

"Using an anecdote about Disneyland, I will explain how you might use this information from the fan survey to create product and service innovations that will pass the bar stool test and strengthen your positioning.

"About a year after Disneyland's grand opening, Walt conducted a survey of guests who were frequent visitors. The objective was to determine what it was that attracted them to the park repeatedly. At that time that the park was in its initial stages of development, the statements that the park was extraordinarily clean and always appeared new topped the list.

"Walt Disney was a genius and practical at the same time. He concluded that his greatest fans were the repeat customers who could clearly see and understand that Disneyland was a family park where cleanliness was an important attractor. This was part of the specific design to make the park a safe and magical experience for young children. He determined that if he could design a system of taking care of the park environment in a way that even less-detail-conscious guests could appreciate the beauty and care taken, Disneyland would generate many more enthusiastic fans. According to the story, it was the inception of Disney's concept to use cleanliness as a strategic customer attractor.

"I haven't verified the story, and it doesn't matter how accurate it is, because the principle is solid and true." Sitting very straight, the Master spoke in a low and deliberate tone, causing John to lean forward and listen closely.

"If you take the mosaic pieces of greatness from your company—as perceived by your customer—and build a powerful system, you will attract many more customers and convert them into fans.

"I suggest taking the strengths of your services and products, as experienced by your fans, and build a service plan. It should pass the bar stool test without much fine-tuning.

"One of the greatest benefits of the fan survey is that it serves as a motivational tool for your sales team, since it is performed *prior* to your coaching program designed to teach them how to deliver five-star service to the clients.

"Most service campaigns are initiated upon reviewing a customer service survey that reported substandard service and requires your team to make improvements. The problem with a campaign like that is that the employees know that they have not performed well, and usually they also know exactly which improvements are needed. It is far more difficult to inspire a *change* in behavior from poor to average or good than it is to inspire the employee *before* the poor patterns have started.

"When we performed the first fan surveys, we were surprised by the striking difference in the degree of motivation initially shown by the sales and service teams. Imagine being a key account manager being invited to present to a group of colleagues the stories of what your greatest fans love most about you and your company. Then, another team member shares one of his greatest successes in customer service. The general level of energy and confidence in the group is elevated. Everyone becomes aware of the strengths generated through this process. Beginning with a strong foundation of motivation and caring, ask how the service systems of the company could be improved so every customer can benefit from the excellent customer service just demonstrated. Watch the interesting phenomenon that takes place. The team will become incredibly creative and present ideas with enthusiasm. They will have the confidence of knowing that these ideas can be realized after witnessing the motivating testimonies of their colleagues. Is that a cool idea or what?" The Master was grinning from ear to ear, clearly still excited by his subject matter after years of dedication and study.

He continued like an excited child. "Would you like to add turbo charge to your strategy to overtake your competitors and accelerate your expert positioning swiftly?"

John nodded excitedly. Initially he had suspected the promises made in this room may have been overestimated and would not be forthcoming. But so far, the Master had not failed to deliver. He finally had hope. With these tools, he felt certain that he could create an impressive, emotionally driven, expert profile from a client's perspective. He couldn't imagine that the concepts could be improved or built upon further, but if the Master promised it, John was excited to see what he would come up with next.

Positioning Exercise No. 5: Building a Prototype

"John, are you familiar with prototypes in automobile design?"

"I believe you are referring to the model designs presented at automobile shows by the manufacturers. Aren't they usually fake, or a shell of the car without the engine?" John was perplexed by the question.

"Yes, that's one kind of prototype. Another one is an exact replica of what the car will look like, built by hand. These prototypes are usually test-driven by the CEO or other top decision-makers to determine whether the new model is worth putting into production. Before the CEO of Daimler-Chrysler, Toyota, or GM decides on investing billions of dollars into new production facilities, they want a clear idea of whether the new S-Class or the new Corvette is worth the effort and expense. The tool to base this decision on is the prototype.

"This is the concept I designed for my clients to use with their customers as well. A prototype is a marvelous tool. It works best for complex products and services when it is not easy for the customer to develop a clear picture of the benefits from a first impression only.

"I invented this instrument and used if for the first time a few years ago when IBM-Germany invited me to coach their most successful dealers in a marketing seminar. I met several times a year with twenty-four of Germany's finest computer programming entrepreneurs to build a powerful marketing concept for each of them. At one meeting, one of the entrepreneurs told me that they had just received new software for workflow processes, logistics, and other key processes in management. The software was capable of assisting Fortune 500 companies, and the license fee for the smallest version was more than $30,000 a month. So this gentleman said to me, 'This is an extremely powerful tool. How can we effectively sell it to our major clients?' I replied, 'Tell me in one sentence what that software can do for me as an entrepreneur and I will show you how to design a sales campaign.'

"Completely bewildered, the man answered, 'You don't understand much about software for workflow processes, do you? Otherwise you would know how complex this is. It's not possible to explain in one sentence what it does.' I said, 'Well, if you can't explain the benefits in one sentence, I can't understand the benefits. And if I don't understand them, I won't buy your product.'

"The gentleman tried again. 'Listen, I know you want a clear and concise picture of the benefits. That's a good sales approach. But it simply won't work here. That software is so complex that you have to open more than 400 windows when you go through the layers.'

"That's really impressive. But I won't buy software to open 400 windows. As an entrepreneur, I buy software if it helps me solve a problem faster, better, or cheaper. So again, tell me one simple thing the software can do better, faster, or cheaper!'

"A bit frustrated, he said, 'Okay, you can reduce the time to order products from your warehouse dramatically.'

"What does dramatically mean in terms of time?' I asked. 'Well, we just did research for a chain of shoe stores. It usually takes the salesperson about fifteen minutes to re-order a certain kind of shoe in a certain size. With our system, the order time is reduced to six minutes.'

"Now we have a deal: You told me about one specific benefit. I will show you how to sell the product. Is it accurate to assume that a salesperson in a shoe store in Germany costs an employer approximately $60.00 an hour, including his salary, health insurance, and all taxes?' The gentleman nodded. 'That's a fairly accurate estimate.'

"'The ordering process currently costs me $15.00, and your software reduces it to $6.00. Is that correct?" Yes. This was the critical point. I knew that the software license was over $30,000 a month. Would this one advantage produce enough savings? I asked the gentleman, 'Tell me how many order processes you have every month.' Without hesitation, he said, 'Between 50,000 and 80,000.'

"I was completely speechless. 'Wait a minute, 50,000 orders multiplied by nine dollars savings per order would amount to $450,000.00 savings per month. You have to ask how to sell something to somebody for $30,000 a month, if they will save $450,000 a month?'

"As if this were a foreign concept, the gentleman and his peers were spellbound. 'It seems so obvious when you put it that way!'

"You see, John, that's the purpose of building prototypes. Reduce complexity and build examples so any layman or twelve-year-old can instantly understand the following things:

1) What monetary results will you have?

2) How much money do you have to invest to achieve these results?"

Looking intently, the Master continued. "Most people understand the concept of prototypes and agree that they are extremely powerful. The advantage to us is that few people act on these insights. I recently conducted a search on the fifty top-ranked Web sites for private health insurance and the fifty top-ranked Web sites for company pension plans. Only five out of these hundred used a prototype on their landing page to describe the monetary benefit of their products.

"To give you another example, I coached one of the leading specialists in our country on company pension plans. I asked him, 'If my employees join your pension plan, what is the advantage for my company?' It took him over two hours to explain to me that such a plan could save me up to $686.00 in taxes for each employee every year. I then asked, 'Well, any tax accountant who understands these concepts could do the same thing for me, and nearly all tax accountants in Germany would understand these concepts. So what makes your plan different?' My client said, 'In theory, that's true. But in Germany, only 8 percent of the employees have such a plan. For the past four years, I have specialized in obtaining this kind of plan for employees. In over 120 companies where we have successfully initiated them, we have an average participation rate of 77 percent, meaning that I sell nearly ten times as many plans to participants as the average tax consultant.'

"'Wow, that's powerful,' I replied. 'Let's put that prototype on the landing page of your Web site, so that anyone shopping for a pension plan will instantly recognize the benefit of doing business with you instead of your competition. That's truly irresistibly attractive positioning!"

Positioning Exercise No. 6: The *Concorde Answer*

"John, have you ever flown on the Concorde from New York to Paris or London in three hours and twenty minutes?" The Marketing Master stood and walked to the window, admiring the beautiful view as he spoke. The sudden change in topics had John wondering what the new exercise would entail.

"No, I dreamt about it, but the company I was working for at that time wouldn't have considered spending that kind of budget in the interest of saving a few hours," John replied.

"Well, the experience itself is much less spectacular than you might imagine. The cabin is small and cramped on the inside. There are two seats on the left and two on the right. Being six feet tall, you wouldn't have been able to stand upright in the aisle.

"The most attractive feature was that the plane's speed was on display throughout the flight. Above the Atlantic, the mach meter showed an impressive 2.4—meaning you were traveling at 2.4 times the speed of sound. Another feature was that Air France served Veuve Cliquot champagne, and that it was often possible to meet wealthy and influential people to network with. This inspired me to develop what I call the *Concorde Answer*:

"Imagine flying the Concorde to Paris and sitting next to a nice fellow who is a very successful businessman. You recognize a potential partner for a joint business venture. After introducing yourself and clinking champagne glasses with your new acquaintance, he asks what you do for a living. ***What answer could you give in one sentence that would entice your new friend into an engaging conversation about your business for the duration of your trip, until you arrive at immigrations in Paris?***

"That answer, given in one sentence—benefit loaded—is the *Concorde Answer*.

"Imagine being a lawyer, sitting in the Concorde and telling your neighbor, 'I'm a lawyer. I love my job. It's pretty exciting.' Most people don't think of law as an exciting or sexy profession. However, if instead you say, 'I teach entrepreneurs to reduce their taxes 60 to 80 percent by setting up international holding accounts,' chances are, you will have his attention. To an entrepreneur, that is sexy!

"Now let's use our marketing consulting company as an example. For years our *Concorde Answer* was 'We teach entrepreneurs to increase their sales by 20 percent in less than ninety days.' Whenever I was invited to a dinner party and I was asked what I do for a living, I took a chance and used our *Concorde Answer.* People often asked if I could guarantee my promise. My response would be, 'No, I can't—not until I know your company intimately. We achieve 20 percent in three months through a professional cross-selling campaign with existing clients. Depending on how consistently you did your homework of high-quality contact management with your clients in the last three years, it may be easy or not so easy to achieve a sales increase of 20 percent. But within a ninety-minute analysis, done in a free consultation, I can determine your potential and tell you what to do to achieve that success rate.'

"Very often, people are so excited and impressed that I obtain a business card and an appointment on the spot. Even when attending the wedding of my personal assistant two years ago, other guests inquired about my profession in friendly conversation. They wanted to know more about the company that the bride worked for. I received four business cards and several appointments, which—at the bottom line—translates into profitability for me and my new clients." The Master sat back comfortably, giving his student a moment to absorb the new information.

"But remember, while the *Concorde Answer* is a wonderful way to open doors, the real value is that it is the 'North Star' of all of your marketing communication:

- The *Concorde Answer* is the first impression and first message a client should get when he accesses your Web site. For example, when you access the Web site of our pension plan expert, his headline reads in bold letters: 'Sell 80 percent of your employees a superior pension plan, and SAVE $686.00 a year per employee."

- The important questions are:
- Is the *Concorde Answer* the first impression made on your company's brochure and Web site?
- Does every flyer communicate the message clearly?
- Is it the main message you relay in public relations interviews?
- Do your display windows, your interior decor, your verbal and your non-verbal messages at the point of sale communicate the Concorde message?
- Does your newsletter convey the Concorde message repeatedly?

"Two of my favorite *Concorde Answers* of all time are messages that world-class companies were built on: 'Domino's Pizza—delivered in thirty minutes or less … or it's free!' and 'Federal Express: When it absolutely, positively has to be there overnight.' When you examine their communication strategies, you will notice that everything they communicate is arranged very carefully around their *Concorde Answer*."

Standing and stretching, the Master indicated the end of the day's lesson.

"Well, it's about noon, John. Lake Starnberg and the inspiring panoramic view of the Bavarian Alps await you. I suggest a three-hour boat trip in this wonderful weather. Don't miss the palace where King Ludwig lived. As you feel inspired, study these six exercises. This will change the course of your company forever. I will see you tomorrow."

John left the Marketing Master's office overwhelmed and intoxicated with new ideas. *I need a break,* he said to himself, walking down to the lake the shortest way possible. A few minutes later, he saw an inviting bench in the park—nicely nestled under the shadow of a big oak tree. *What a place for a little nap,* he thought, putting himself to a peaceful rest.

When John woke up, it was close to sunset. "Wow, a two-hour nap on a park bench—that hasn't happened for years! It must be the jet lag," he chuckled, feeling completely refreshed. "I'll spoil myself with another latte macchiato."

Sipping his latte, he opened his diary to put down what he had learned that day:

- Perspective is the key to perception. Looking at my company from the perspective of my customer's heart is the most powerful strategic focus point.
- That way I can look and feel beyond the technical standards of my industry. Delivering good products and services is the standard of all good competitors in our field—becoming uniquely lovable is the extra mile that leads to success.
- The bar stool test will tell us how good the story is. As long as our customers will not talk about it, we have not moved them emotionally because what people are emotional about, they talk about.
- We'll do a fan survey. The customers who already like us the most are the ones who will tell us where we are lovably unique and different.
- When we take their feedback as puzzle pieces and put them together, the picture of our emotional profile will appear.
- Fine-tuning that picture and celebrating these emotional touches with all our customers will help us—the way Walt Disney did—to win even more customers' hearts!
- Building prototypes and explaining the benefits of our services in a measurable way will set us apart from the competition. Clients really want to know "WIIIFM"—what is in it for me? If we can answer that using a short example, we are far ahead.
- Boiling down the prototype into a *Concorde Answer* will serve us as the guiding star of our PR and customer communication. From Christmas cards to our Web page, we will tell them the benefit of doing business with us in one sentence—"hot, fresh, delivered in less than thirty minutes or it's free."

Chapter 3: The Second Heart Magnet—Trust-building through Word of Mouth

John was awake at the crack of dawn with no need for an alarm. It was five AM when his feet touched the floor.

He had worked until midnight listing the new ideas he had learned about expert positioning. Sleep had been elusive. His dreams had been interrupted by the outstanding information he had received from the Master. If the information about building trust through word of mouth that he would learn today could be even half as useful as the information he had already gained, he could transform his business in no time.

The promise of possibility prompted him to arrive fifteen minutes early. The Master, seeing him looking refreshed and ready for the lesson ahead, said, "Good morning, John. You're early. You must be eager for the information that will help you and your clients excel to new levels."

"You certainly know how to make a person feel welcome. I am ready and eager." John smiled. It didn't go unnoticed that the Master greeted John personally, even though he had several assistants and staff in the office. These personal touches made John feel very important and special as a client. "I noticed that you greet me personally each day. Is this one of the principles of Heartselling?"

"I'm happy that you noticed. I truly believe that Heartselling is selling from your heart to the customer's heart. So if you—as the business owner—are not genuinely interested in your clients and your intention and attention—the most powerful forces in the universe—are not directed to serve your customers, your business will not flourish in the long run, and even the marketing tools we discuss here won't serve you. As an old Chinese proverb already stated thousands of years ago, 'If you don't know how to smile, don't open a business.' I truly believe that the quality of a heart-driven life is always and easily outperforming the quality of a mind-driven life. So being with my clients the way I am is really not driven by strategies or techniques, it is driven by who I am.

"Being fully present when you are with any person, and allowing them to feel that they are special and worthy of your time and attention enables you to focus your heart and mind on that person. This is true whether that person is your wife, a client, or a stranger on a plane. You will carry your love and identification with you and through you. That is more valuable than any marketing campaign.

"Being leads to doing, and doing leads to success and results. While many entrepreneurs know this in theory, oftentimes they ignore the importance of this revelation when it comes to marketing campaigns. They still believe the key to success is a larger budget and a more elaborate marketing campaign.

"But the truth is different. The reality is that the most effective marketing campaigns are often extremely cost-efficient. It is more important to have a brilliant idea and the patience to implement it than to have a lavish marketing budget without creativity and passion. The most successful entrepreneurs don't focus on getting more money for their marketing efforts, but rather focus on being present with their clients and responding to their needs with creative solutions.

"Perhaps the best way to demonstrate this is word of mouth. Every entrepreneur and manager knows there is not a single instrument in marketing, advertising, or sales as powerful or effective as word of mouth. There is no other tool that can buy you more new clients with a smaller budget than word of mouth. The best thing about it is that it is underrated and not well understood, leaving those of us who master it with little competition. Most so-called marketing experts have three major distortions in their mental maps when it comes to word of mouth:

1. They do not effectively use it with the right people. They believe that when it comes to word of mouth, all customers are equal—which is a huge misconception.

2. They believe word of mouth is not in their sphere of influence because it happens in their absence when clients talk to each other. This is incorrect. Word of mouth *is* in the entrepreneur's sphere of influence, and *can*—and often *should* happen in his or her presence.

3. The majority of entrepreneurs don't understand the development of piggyback networking and other word-of-mouth principles that have been developed and proven to be extremely powerful in the last ten years."

Word-of-Mouth Strategy No. 1: Start with the right people

"John, did you know that social scientists discovered over a decade ago that human beings in a group are connected with each other through a few members of the group called the *communication channels?* There are only a few of these people in each group."

"I've never heard that," John admitted. "Social psychology always seemed boring to me. I always thought they overstated the obvious and dressed it up in scientific terms."

"There may be some truth to that, but with their insights on communication channels, we could make millions. Let's look at the simplicity of the meaning 'communication channels.'

"Think back to high school, specifically to when you returned after the summer holidays. Recall a new student joining your class; maybe his father worked for the American Embassy. How was he introduced to your class? Did all thirty students in the class go to meet him during the first break, or were there a couple students (even at age fifteen) who made the first move, who befriended the new student and introduced him to the rest of the class?"

"In my class with twenty-eight students, there may have been four or five students with a personality like that … people I would call *connectors*," John replied.

"That's exactly what research shows. I was discussing this topic a few months ago at our Thanksgiving dinner. My wife had invited the kindergarten teachers from my son's school. When I told them about this research, they looked surprised.

"One of the teachers responded, 'You can witness this behavior long before children are fifteen. Come to our kindergarten class and watch our group. Even with four- and five-year-olds, it is very apparent who facilitates the process of group interaction, ensuring a new child is integrated into the group.'

"I have no scientific evidence for it," the Master continued, "but I don't have a shadow of a doubt that these teachers are correct. Are you getting excited yet?" The Master had a teasing twinkle in his eye. "Do you see how we could make tons of money with that insight alone?"

"That would be great, but how can I capitalize on that in my word-of-mouth campaigns?"

"Easily, John; what these social psychologists and kindergarten teachers have in common is that the 'Pareto law' holds true when it comes to word of mouth. Are you familiar with Vilfredo Pareto?"

"Of course I know him. He's the Italian economist who discovered that cause-and-effect relationships in systems are not linear. Usually 20 percent or less of the elements in a given system produce the majority, often more than 80 percent of the results. This seems to hold true in the area of income distribution, where Pareto researched it. I know it because 30 percent of my salespeople produce close to three-quarters of our results. The insurance companies know it because 20 percent of all drivers cause the majority of all accidents."

"That's exactly right!" the Marketing Master complimented John. "Although it is often overlooked in the area of word of mouth, the Pareto principle holds true there as well. ***Less than 20 percent of your customers produce 80 percent or more of your word of mouth!***

"If you have two hundred clients, approximately forty of them will likely be 'people connectors.' You can determine this by analyzing your circle of friends. Out of ten of your closest friends, chances are that one or two always know what's cool and new, where to buy what. If not, they know where to find the information. Whenever you chat with them, it doesn't take long before they have a recommendation for you.

"Now, imagine—as some of my clients have done in the past—you invite one people connector from your group of clients per week for lunch to discuss ideas of business cooperation. Instead of inviting 200 clients over a period of four years and receiving 170 rejections to obtain 30 positive responses, you could have 40 high-yield meetings in less than a year, finding 30 partners interested in cooperation. Our field tests show that three out of four people from a group of connectors say yes when you suggest an appropriate kind of cooperation. Would that be cool or would that be cool?" the Marketing Master asked, probing with another "yes-or-yes-question."

"That would be wonderful, but how do I determine who these people connectors are from my group of clients?" John couldn't conceal the excitement in his voice.

"Would you be able to spot one of these talented and motivated social networkers from your tennis club if you saw them?" the Master asked.

"It's pretty obvious. If you pay attention to how guests behave at social gatherings, you can quickly determine the people connectors."

"Great, then just get out your client list and scan your 'A' and 'B' lists. Who does your intuition tell you are the people connectors?"

John took his Palm organizer and went through his electronic Rolodex. The Marketing Master was correct. In those cases where he knew the clients, it was easy to imagine them as "people connectors" as far back as kindergarten, helping to integrate and manage groups.

"Okay, where I know my clients, it's easy to visualize. In cases where I'm not familiar with them, I can ask my sales team. But what do we do once we have identified our word-of-mouth team? How do we activate them?"

"I will share five practical ways to initiate word of mouth. You can learn from the mistake many of my clients made in the past. These techniques are precision tools and work extremely well with the right clients—people connectors. If you overdo it and try to use them with all of your customers, you will get frustrated."

Word-of-Mouth Strategy No. 2: Five ways of initiating word of mouth

a. Event marketing with people connectors

"It may be different with American companies, but most of my European clients do not show adequate return on investment from their event marketing. Even with lavish events costing hundreds of thousands of dollars, they measure up poorly when determining the number of prospects gained from the event. Here is an example.

"A client of mine, one of the most prestigious German private banks, hired my firm to develop a new marketing concept. I was told that they were doing some of the finest event marketing in town, and this event was the talk of the town in Munich for weeks.

"They had rented the castle of Possenhofen at Lake Starnberg, one of the most prestigious castles in Bavaria. The last princess of Austria was known to spend her summer vacations there. They hired the best caterer in Munich. The main speaker was Mr. Illbruck, a world-champion skipper who won multiple Olympic gold medals. The guest list was an exclusive, hand-selected list of the 100 to 150 most financially successful families in Bavaria. They had been holding outstanding events like this every spring and fall for three years.

"When I asked them how many new clients they received with this kind of networking event, there was a moment of silence. The CEO was the first to respond. 'We haven't received one customer with this approach yet.'

"I was speechless. I knew it was possible to do a really poor job in networking … but to have received not one customer from such lavish events over a time span of three years seemed impossible. I asked the CEO, 'Which circle of clients did you invite to those events?' He answered, 'We didn't invite any of our customers. We only invited high-class potentials because this was strictly an event to win new customers.'

"John, can you imagine being invited there? Maybe you were interested in finding a new financial advisor. As you were standing at the buffet with other potential clients, you ask, 'How long have you been working with this bank?'

The first person might answer, 'I'm not a client. I came because I enjoy sailing. When I heard that Mr. Illbruck was going to be here, I decided to come. What about you? How long have you worked with their team of financial advisors, and how well did they do during the last economic downturn?'—'Well, I can't really tell you. I'm not a client either. Like you, I came to meet the world-class athlete, Mr. Illbruck.'

"What do you think, John? A hundred fifty people meet and stand around a beautiful buffet, discussing the performances of their financial advisors. None was a client of the inviting bank. Would you like to bet that there was a lot of word of mouth going around that night for the competition?"

"So I coached my client to avoid three main mistakes in the future when doing event marketing:

- Don't present the main speaker or the main show before the social gathering. Some of the interesting prospects may leave after lunch or dinner. Always frame the social gathering by top presenters.
- Never ever offer a buffet. It is one of the greatest handicaps for your salespeople. Always have your guests sit down at round tables and feed them a three- or four-course meal.
- Never allow free seating. Always have a perfectly devised seating plan.

"With these simple rules, you will know immediately when you access a conference room whether this event lends itself to powerful word of mouth. When you see round tables and nametags directing people to sit next to one another, chances are the event is orchestrated well and will be a huge success.

"Experts will arrange the event this way:

- Open the event with a 'bang' by having a well-known speaker or another highlight to attract the attention of the audience.
- Have the first speaker announce the highlights of the event and the schedule following the meals.
- Put at least two or three of your 'word-of-mouth' clients at each table.
- Mix three or four top prospects at each table with your word-of-mouth clients.
- Seat one sales agent at that table with instructions not to interfere with your word-of-mouth clients, who will be more effective at selling to your prospects than your sales agent would be. (This is not a reflection of the skill of the sales agent, but the fact that he is not perceived as being as independent or objective as your networking people, who are active clients.)
- You should place as much priority on the seating arrangement of this event as you would on your daughter's wedding reception. If you don't set the stage for word of mouth to ignite, it will not happen magically.
- Your sales agents should be prepared to augment the conversation only in the rare occurrence that the people connectors are not performing well that day. The agents should have questions prepared to ignite the conversation. An example of such a question would be, 'Mr. Muller, do you recall if it was in 2003 or 2004 that we doubled your stock portfolio in less than six months?'"

Grinning at John, who was furiously taking notes, the Master added, "I have conducted small events with as few as three tables of eight people, each seating two or three networking clients, three or four prospects, and a few salespeople. Within sixty to ninety minutes, during a meal, with a total of twelve prospects present, we are usually able to yield an average of ten or eleven consultations. At a highly successful event, we may even get all twelve of them to commit to the next appointment. These intimate events cost a fraction of what the larger, more prestigious events cost, and typically bring more business to our clients. While not as glamorous or prestigious, they are more functional and provide a better stage for intelligent networking and successful use of word-of-mouth strategies."

b. Presenting people connectors for public appearances

"Years ago, I learned another effective method to systematically integrate powerful word-of-mouth strategies. A colleague of mine was giving sixty-to-ninety-minute dinner presentations to local Rotary and marketing club members in large cities around his area. I attended one of his events to hear his speech. Suddenly my colleague was surprised to discover three of his regular clients in the last row. Happy to see them, he capitalized on the moment by inviting them on stage to share with the audience how the strategies he was discussing that night (and that these customers were already implementing) were already effectively improving their business. At the completion of the speech, out of the thirty-two participants, eighteen gave him their business card. I congratulated him on his wonderful speech and inquired about the nice word-of-mouth element with his active clients in the middle of his presentation.

"He explained to me how he discovered the power of this technology by accident several years before, when several of his satisfied clients unwittingly attended one of his events. He spontaneously had the idea to invite them on stage to give a one-minute testimonial. As a result, he received three times more business cards than usual. From that time on, he began planting two or three of his fans in the audience. Often, they are willing to do it without charging a fee, in appreciation of his efforts that led to their success, but sometimes he offers to pay for their assistance. It has been one of the most profitable marketing moves he ever initiated."

c. Word-of-mouth telephone conferences

"Another way to inject word of mouth into your company's communication with a small budget is through telephone conferences. I learned this incredibly valuable technique from a large pharmaceutical company that has been a long-time client of mine.

"I found it interesting to discover that they were the first of my large clients to institutionalize word of mouth in their marketing plan and to actually include a budget for it. They were so successful with this strategy and kept it so covert that even I had a hard time discovering their secret to success, though this is my expertise.

"Their basic approach to introducing a new medication to the market was to look for early adapts among physicians who had had great results with patients they had treated with this medication. As soon as they had generated a few fans for the new product, they organized a roll-out series of phone conferences across the nation. Their sales associates invited skeptical physicians to participate in a telephone conference with fifty to a hundred participants. During this conference, a moderator invited several of the physicians who were fans and had had excellent results with the product to tell their colleagues about their experience. This was the most effective and efficient way to spread word of mouth rapidly."

"It's hard to believe that three satisfied customers could effectively convince fifty to a hundred skeptical physicians," John interrupted. "What I know from discussions even in our tennis club is that when you are in the minority, you often lose a discussion, even though you can prove your arguments."

"You have a good point," the Marketing Master nodded in agreement. "That's exactly how group dynamics function in discussion circles. If the majority believes something, it's extremely difficult for a small minority to sway the beliefs of the rest of the group, with one important exception: ***Psychologists found when analyzing marketing focus groups in the 1970s that if the minority experienced something directly with their five senses, no force in the world could talk them out of it, and they could easily persuade the majority on a regular basis.***

"Let's say you are a Porsche enthusiast and are invited to test drive the new Porsche Turbo on the world famous Nurburgring. You sit next to Rally world champion Walter Röhrl, and you clock his lap time at seven minutes, forty-five seconds. You tell this to your friends at home in the L.A. Porsche Club, who have never heard of anyone lapping the ring in a street Porsche at a speed faster than nine minutes, thirty seconds. If you had experienced it in person, seen it, felt it, maybe even taken a video of it, there would be no discussion about the possibility of it having been done. You would convince 99 percent of the people present of the truth of what you witnessed.

"The formula for word-of-mouth phone conference is:

- Invite all the new clients you want to inform about the new product.
- Invite clients who already believe in your new product and are excited to share their experience.
- Have a moderator, preferably someone neutral, not from your company. A good example would be a well-known author on this subject to do the interviewing.
- Set up a budget for this type of marketing campaign and make sure that your salespeople invite all relevant customers to these word-of-mouth conferences."

d. Cleaning the staircase from top to bottom

"So far we've looked at your opportunities for initiating word of mouth from the point of communication channels. Since 20 percent of your clients will do 80 percent of your word of mouth, they are the easiest and most rewarding group to start with.

"Another catalytic group to use for word of mouth is opinion leaders. Imagine that you live in a small town where a lot of people know the mayor, the priest of your church, the most successful car dealer, and some other respected authorities, and you succeed to win them over as clients for your gardening business. There's a good chance that it will become known throughout town that it was your company that provided the service to these high-profile clients. You can design a powerful sales campaign, spreading word of mouth around such opinion leaders.

"Years ago, a very successful real estate agent taught me this strategy. He was the most successful agent in a team of over 250 salespeople, outperforming his competition by a landslide. Mesmerized by his success, I inquired about his secret. Smiling, he went on to tell me the story.

"'Years ago, a middle manager at Porsche in Stuttgart wanted to buy a condominium from me and I said no!'

"Curious, I told him he had my undivided attention with this unconventional approach, and asked to explain how he became the top salesperson by rejecting sales. With a grin, he continued. 'I said no to the head of that department. Six months later, I sold an exclusive estate to the CEO of Porsche. Several months after that, I was referred by him to a director at Bosch, the company that delivers the electronic units for Porsches. From there, a recommendation to the CEO of Blaupunkt, a subsidiary of Bosch ... and the domino effect continued. When I analyzed the chain of recommendations, which led to more than ten sales in two years, I discovered a deep truth about business: **The staircase is always cleaned from top to bottom!'**—'I'm not sure I follow you.' This was a new concept to me.

"'If I had started selling real estate at the level of middle management, as I did years ago, I never ever would have become a trusted advisor to the CEO and his board of directors. I never would have gotten all these high-quality recommendations in the automotive industries. CEOs know CEOs. Directors know directors. It's as simple as that. Knowing this, I **think of markets as communication communities.** Consider painters. Each region of the country has a chamber of commerce where all different branches of craftsmen are organized. The chamber of commerce in Munich, for example, lists over 500 painting companies. To you and me, they are one anonymous group. But within the group, it's a fairly small community, and everyone knows the three or five most successful companies in that region. To get an appointment with the owner of these successful companies is difficult. But after selling to one or two of the top people in the organization, my assistant calls all painters from top to bottom and spreads the word of mouth that the *top dog* does business with me because I developed a special offer for this industry. That's my only secret: I define a market as a communication community, sell to the opinion leaders first, then spread word of mouth myself down the staircase from top to bottom.'"

John was impressed. "I didn't think you could do much to enhance word of mouth except maybe pray," he said with enthusiasm. "Now I see a myriad of possibilities." Nodding in agreement, the Master added, "That's only the beginning. The best is yet to come."

e. Injecting Word of Mouth into the decision-making process

"How can you grow your company faster without increasing the number of salespeople, the closing ratio, or the number of recommendations per client?" the Marketing Master asked John.

"That sounds like a Japanese koan, one of those questions you can meditate over for years and never come up with an answer for. As long as you have the same number of customers, the same number of recommendations, and the same closing ratio, in my book of experience, there is no way to grow faster and bring in more sales."

"Sounds logical, but it's wrong," came the clipped response. "Imagine a market for paper-production machines in Germany, where every year one hundred large printing machines are sold. Furthermore, you are one of five suppliers in this market, and every competitor has a market share of 20 percent, which means selling twenty of these large printers in a year. Our last assumption is that the clients will take an average of twelve months to make their decision on these investments of a couple of million dollars.

"Let's say you outperform your competition and do everything to accelerate your clients' decision-making processes. You are the first in the industry to develop a due-diligence process for this kind of investment, which is exactly what we did for one of my clients a few years ago. All the information a client needs and wants, you put into one simple process. After three years of fine-tuning that decision-making process, your clients are able to make their decision within six months instead of a year.

"This means that your share of twenty prospects will have made their decision by the end of June instead of by the end of the year, which will allow you to find another twenty clients to close from July to December. That year you will have gained forty new clients out of a market of one hundred prospects. Your competitors will have been left with fifteen customers each. After three years of doing this, you would have 120 new clients, while each of your competitors would have 45 during the same time period. Is that cool or cool?"

"That is extremely cool," John agreed, "but how can you accelerate the decision-making process on your clients' side so dramatically?"

"There are two main cards you could play," the Master explained. "The first is to make sure that all information you offer to your client during the decision-making process is optimized for the client to decide. That means you will educate your client about his options as clearly as possible and help him reduce the complexity. A good model is the due-diligence process consultants use during merger-and-acquisition projects. You can chew on the numbers of a huge company for years and never really know the value of the company. Or you can follow a structured evaluation process and be ready to make a decision within eight weeks.

"The second card you can play, one I highly recommend, is to use word of mouth as a decision accelerator during the last phase, before the decision is made. That is one of the most successful ways to implement word of mouth.

Clients go through two phases when making decisions:

- the information phase
- the verification phase."

Walking to the diagram board, the Master drew a picture. "It looks something like this."

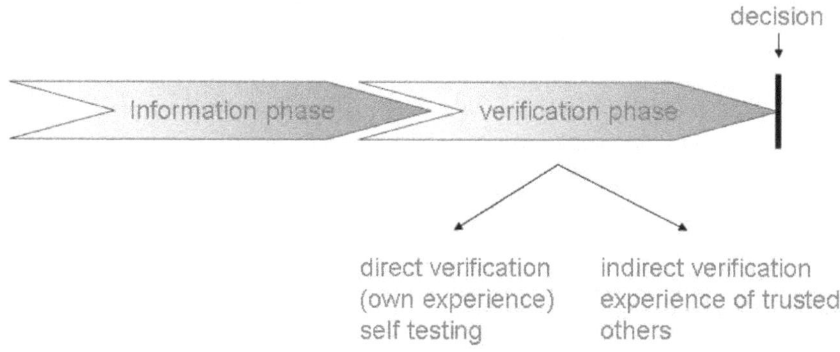

"Before we can make a decision, we need some information so that we know what basis to decide on. First, BMW has to describe the new 507-horsepower M5 model before you can start dreaming and getting excited about having it as a company car. After reading the brochure, you move to the second phase of the decision-making process, described by psychologists as *verification.* This is when you verify that the promises made by BMW about their product are true. You do this by direct or indirect experience. You experience it for yourself, or trust the experience of someone else. A common mistake of many entrepreneurs is that *they believe that regarding decision-making, most of their clients would prefer direct experience to indirect experience.*

"Think about this concept for a moment: If you are shopping for a new laptop, would you drive to the electronics store on Saturday morning, take your James Bond DVD, and ask the salesperson to demonstrate the screen quality of fifteen laptops so you can make a substantiated decision three hours later? Or would you prefer to trust the trained expert working in the store, or call a friend who works in the IT department who specializes in evaluating laptops for your sales team and ask for his advice?"

"I would ask my friend from the IT department," John agreed. "Not only would this save time, but computers are complex. I could easily buy an inferior product, even though it may appear to have the best picture when playing the movie."

"Most people would agree with you," the Master said, nodding. "And there are some products that simply everybody will agree nobody would like to have direct experience with. Life insurance is an example. You would have to be dead in order to find out whether the company really pays your family when you die. This is a dramatic example, but it illustrates a major point in selling services. Whether it's your financial advisor, a contractor who is building your home, or a new tax consultant, these are those types of services whose value may only be discovered when it is too late.

"People prefer to take calculated and informed risks when making decisions. The most reliable way to do that is through others who have already taken the risk and can give feedback based on experience.

The more important and complex the decision is, the more valuable word of mouth becomes to the client.

"If this truth is so easily discovered, why isn't word of mouth utilized as a primary tool by professionals selling expensive services? It seems logical to use this tool as an accelerator in the decision-making process. Either it is unknown to the competition, as unlikely as that seems, or they are generously giving us the edge." The Master scratched his chin and smiled sarcastically.

"Regardless of your field and who your client is, once you've made your offer to the client and have given him all the information he needs to make an informed decision, that would be the time to connect your client with other clients who are currently fans of the product you are selling. An example might be buying a car—like the BMW from our last example. Nearly all prospects thinking of making a substantial investment will be interested in talking to a current consumer of the product. That is the perfect time for you to set up a phone conference.

"The secret is, once you introduce your prospect to a few of your customers, you excuse yourself. Here's an example: 'I'm sorry, Mr. Jones, but I will have to ask you to excuse me. My boss left to take a customer for a test drive, and there's another customer waiting. Why don't you talk to Mr. Smith at your leisure in private, and I will return as quickly as possible.'

"We have tested the next step dozens of times. As soon as you leave the customer alone during the phone conference, the prospect will ask the fan to be totally honest and tell him about the downside of the product. ***We need to be able to assess the pros and cons against one another to make an informed decision. As long as we don't have an objective picture of the cons (we assume that the company selling the item will clearly inform us of the benefits), we consciously or subconsciously refuse to make a decision.***

"So don't be afraid that the fan might say something negative about the product. ***Providing the opportunity for the client to discover—through word of mouth—what he subconsciously needed to know is often the most powerful decision accelerator you can use.***

"It is a real service for your client; it accelerates the growth of your business, and because it's so rarely used, it's an opportunity for you to outshine your competition."

Word-of-Mouth Strategy No. 3: Developing a Heart-Touching Story

"Do you ever shop for perfumes for your wife?" the Master asked.

"Funny you should ask. I just bought a bottle of Chanel No. 5 at the airport last week when I was returning from a business trip."

"Did you have it gift-wrapped?"

"Yes, actually the clerk offered me the choice of a dozen different wrapping papers. I chose my wife's favorite color, and they added a beautiful matching bow."

"Are you aware that the production cost of fifty milliliters of perfume is usually under a dollar? The glass flacon it is presented in typically costs between $9.00 and $12.00 to produce."

"No, I had no idea." John found this concept intriguing. He had assumed that perfume was very expensive, because of the mystique surrounding it. "You mean the packaging costs ten times more than the production of the product itself?"

"That's precisely what I mean. The expensive flacon is put in a prestigious paper box and wrapped in fancy cellophane. Then you come in and purchase the product, and would like it gift-wrapped. So they wrap it in something personalized for the person you are presenting it to. For a really special occasion, you may even add an expensive gift topper, such as a flower arrangement or another small gift. Why do you suppose all this effort goes into the purchase of a quarter cup of scented water?"

"Well, I guess it demonstrates the value of the product and the value of the present, and ultimately our appreciation for the person we present it to!"

"That's a thoughtful answer. But the perfume already comes in a designer bottle, box, and wrapping. So why do people feel the need for further wrapping?"

"My best answer would be that the first packaging shows the value of the product, and the individual wrapping shows my appreciation for my wife," John explained, unable to determine where the Master was heading with this line of questioning.

"You just touched on the concept I'm going to introduce now. Many companies forget this concept when it comes to offering their products and services.

"We can wrap our products physically or mentally with stories to enhance their perceived value. We can then wrap them again when we deliver them to our clients, showing our appreciation for the client. Both wrappings can and often will touch the buyer's heart. And, according to the German proverb I mentioned earlier, 'What the heart is filled with, the mouth is talking about!'"

"I understand what you say about physical wrapping, because it's obvious. I'm not sure I grasp what you mean about mental wrapping through stories."

"Let's analyze physical wrapping for a moment. It is obvious when it comes to product packaging. But outside of that, it's a poorly understood field for most entrepreneurs. The founders of McKinsey have built an image of trust that their company continues to be known for today. At their inception, consultants didn't have a good reputation." With a sarcastic grin and arched brows, the Master continued. "Lawyers were known as advocates for their clients' interests—knowledgeable, correct, and upholding the highest standards. So the founders of McKinsey came up with the brilliant idea of building their offices exactly the way law practices were designed. In other words, they wrapped their service of business consulting with the conservative and trustworthy aura they borrowed from the image of law firms.

- Nike Town and Starbucks wrap their products and services with inviting, positive, and emotionally grabbing environments that make people want to be there and tell their friends as well.
- Some three-star restaurants present their menus in high-class leather binders, drawing more business as a result. We used that simple approach when developing a business plan for a spa

resort. We produced the most exquisite photo documentation we have ever done. It resembled an advertising brochure for a seven-star hotel in Dubai. We have never presented such a small number of brochures with that many graphs, diagrams, and pictures. They were encased in quality leather binders for each participant. The results were outstanding. One decision-maker commented that he had never seen a presentation like that, that it was almost as if he could already see the finished product. He invested immediately, because the desire to take his family there for vacation was vivid in his mind and heart.

"Now let's look at some unique examples for wrapping stories around products and services to enhance word of mouth.

- Years ago, when visiting Stockholm, I went to have a beer at an airport bar. At the entrance was a sign that I will not forget. It read something to the effect of, '*All our drinks are served with original glacier ice from Greenland. Research shows that it's the purest and cleanest ice on the planet. The oxygen encapsulated in this ice is over 4,000 years old, from the time the Egyptians built the pyramids. Pay only $10.00 and the drink of your choice is free.*' I not only had a drink with the purest ice on the planet, which didn't taste any different, by the way, but I told most of my friends when they asked me about my vacation.

- One of our clients, a financial advisor specializing in retirement planning, has developed really powerful concepts in this area of expertise. He received a few recommendations from his clients, but never seemed to grow beyond that regarding word of mouth. For his twenty-fifth business anniversary, he recruited us to design a special campaign for him. We rented three pairs of premium business cars: the S-Class from Mercedes, the 7 Series from BMW, and the A8 from Audi. One was brand new, the other ones two years old but being prepared for resale and appearing new. We invited all his guests to participate in a quiz. Each participant was to guess which of the cars was new and which were a year old. Very few participants guessed correctly on all three vehicle types. The gift for the participants who guessed correctly was a romantic weekend for two at a luxury hotel in the Mediterranean, all expenses paid. At the end of the event, the guest of honor gave a speech. This was his message: 'Most of you are in your forties. Most of you purchase luxury vehicles similar to the ones in our quiz at an average of once in two years. In doing so, you lose $40,000.00 in depreciation. If instead you would purchase a pre-owned vehicle, and sell it when the vehicle is four years old, you would only lose $20,000.00 in depreciation. If you purchase another twelve cars before you retire, you would save $240,000.00 through intelligent shopping, and neither you nor your neighbor would know the difference. Let me show you how you could turn that $240,000.00 into $750,000.00 over the next twenty-five years and have a wonderful pension plan, without sacrificing a single dollar to build it.' The results of that presentation were beyond our wildest expectations. Our client didn't present the rest of the numbers the way he usually would in a typical presentation. But building them into a memorable experience had people talking about it. He had more business from word of mouth in the following year than he had received in the previous twenty-five years.

- There is an elegant Austrian hotel known for offering five-star services and being family-oriented. One of the amenities is the child-sitting program they offer while the parents enjoy leisure time in their gorgeous spa. One of their highlights was taking the mostly metropolitan-raised youths to local farms and teaching them things they were totally foreign to, like milking cows or horseback riding. They were already doing a wonderful job before they hired me to develop a word-of-mouth campaign for them. After some brainstorming—inspired by my own children, who only traveled with their teddy bears—we zeroed in on the fact that most small children brought their bears and dolls along on vacation. We instructed the chambermaids to hide the teddy bears when they cleaned the rooms during breakfast time. We explained to them not to hide the dolls completely, but rather in a teasing way. For example, an arm of a doll would stick out from under the pillow. The next day, the bear would sit under the mirror in the bathroom, decorated

> with a toothbrush. By the second day, the kids were running to the rooms after breakfast, looking for their stuffed animals and dolls. On departure day, we instructed the chambermaids to put a little chocolate heart around the bear's or doll's neck and leave a little note saying, 'Hi, Annie, it was so nice to have you here. Will you come back and visit me again with your teddy bear? Yours, Mary.' Think about it. If you had a wonderful vacation and this happened to your three-year-old daughter, and the teddy bear she loves above everything, would you talk about that experience when back home? Would that story pass the bar stool test?"

Taking a deep breath and processing this information, John paused from his rapid note-taking. "So what you are saying is that good entrepreneurs are constantly thinking about how they can touch their customers' hearts with little stories and gestures. It seems to be the same concept as with Christmas presents. Usually we are not moved most by the most expensive present. We usually receive the most joy from the one with the most meaning and intention from the person we love."

"You seem to understand," the Master confirmed. "When you develop stories and gestures around your products and services, so your clients really feel your appreciation for them and your intention to serve them best, you will benefit from extensive word of mouth."

Word-of-Mouth Strategy No. 4: Piggyback Networking

"John, would you be interested in a word-of-mouth strategy that could deliver hundreds or even thousands of qualified new leads to you in an instant?"

"Naturally, I would," John said. He was wondering what the Master could possibly be thinking of. If the master had dared to make such a promise from the beginning, John would have assumed he had no idea what he was doing and would be unable to deliver on his promises. *But I would most likely have been wrong,* he thought. *So far, everything he has come up with has been common sense. But maybe there is nothing less common than common sense when it comes to marketing.* He said, "Now that I know you better, I really believe that such a strategy may even exist, but I wouldn't have the slightest idea how it might work."

"That's the reason for this discussion about the Seven Magnets of Heartselling. The piggyback networking will be one of the most powerful tools at your disposal. There is no other technique that has helped to make as much money for our clients. Let me walk you through an example, if that is okay." John nodded in agreement and the Master started.

"What we will be talking about here is cooperation between companies. I know that this topic has a bad reputation with entrepreneurs, because the huge majority of these cooperation projects fail. The reason they fail, I would like to point out, is that losers who have no clients themselves connect with other losers who have no clients either. And each of them thinks that if they can attract the business of the other loser first, then a lot of the non-existent clients of their partner will buy from them. This view is flawed from the start." The Master paused for a second before he went on to explain.

"The most important prerequisite is that each partner is already an accepted expert in his field and has strong positioning. The next essential prerequisite is that both experts serve the same target group of customers, but that their products and services are distinctively different. The third and last prerequisite is that every party can offer products and services to his or her partner that are essentially helpful and supportive, to deepen the bond between this expert and his customers.

"Let's imagine we want to open a gourmet food store in Munich. We want to offer over two hundred different types of French cheese, Italian ham smoked in Parma, twenty-five different olive oils, etc. Our plan would be to start our business with huge crowds of highly qualified customers, and the best part of our plan is that it all should cost us close to nothing. Do we agree on the plan so far?"

"It sounds too good to be true … because it is totally unrealistic," John replied with a huge grin.

"You'll see," the Master promised, with the childlike grin John was becoming familiar with. "Let's analyze prerequisite number one: finding an expert in a different branch who serves the same target group that we do. Let's say we find a butcher here in Munich who offers the best-quality meat, serves the crème de la crème, has a great reputation, and can afford to charge 10 percent more than all his competitors because his meat quality is that superb. We visit him and ask whether he is interested in customer loyalty. It's a rhetorical question that we know the answer to. He nods. We ask if he is interested in having us support his customer loyalty program with $30,000.00. 'Isn't it a little early to be drinking?' he asks.

"'Give us two minutes to present our offer. Then you may decide whether we are serious and whether the concept is interesting to you. Is that fair? You have had so many loyal customers for so many years. Wouldn't it be a good idea to say thank you to your one thousand most valuable customers? Imagine giving each of them a voucher for thirty dollars to buy the most exquisite gourmet food Munich has to offer. Maybe you want to write a letter, something like the following:

Dear Mr. and Mrs. Miller,

For over ten years, you have been loyal customers of ours. We appreciate your business more than you may imagine. We would like to thank you for giving us the opportunity to serve you week after week with the finest meat Munich has to offer.

Since the last holiday season, we have cooperated with John's Specialties, Munich's number one gourmet food store. John carries over 200 different kinds of French cheese. Each and every one is a true culinary delight.

To thank you for being our clients, we have reserved a gourmet gift basket at John's with your name on it. Please take this voucher for thirty dollars and select the specialties of your choice. We are so happy to have you as our clients.

Warmest regards,

Paul Hartmann,

Munich's number one address for fine meat quality.'

"What do you think, John? Would it be helpful for Paul's butcher business to thank his one thousand best clients with a thirty-dollar voucher?"

"It would definitely show customer appreciation; most likely his customers would greatly appreciate him in return. Even the customers who don't visit the gourmet store to redeem the voucher will be thankful for the great offer their butcher made to them."

"That's absolutely true," the Marketing Master agreed. "We have done a few dozen campaigns like this for our clients. Whenever they offer real value to their clients—for example, vouchers between twenty and fifty dollars—so the clients can freely select what they want without having to spend their own money, three out of four German customers take advantage of this offer.

"If (and we tested this) the butcher gave away thirty-dollar vouchers for his own products himself, the number of people taking advantage goes down considerably. And if he does it as unintelligently as a lot of companies do, meaning the thirty-dollar voucher is valid only with a hundred-dollar purchase, the customer's interest goes down the tubes.

"Now let's do the numbers. Here's my calculator," the Master said, handing his little pocket computer to John. "We actually did this concept just the way I described it to you, and about 700 of the butcher's customers visited the gourmet shop. Interestingly, nobody bought goods for exactly thirty dollars. Germans hate to look greedy, especially in front of their neighbors. So the average purchase was slightly above fifty-four dollars. Let's assume there is a 140 percent mark-up on the gourmet food. That means we buy it for $100.00, add $140.00 to it, and sell it for $240.00. That means a purchase for $30.00 costs us only $12.50. So please tell me: What is 700 times 12.50?"

"It's a total of $8,750.00," John quickly calculated.

"Now let's look at the $24.00 of additional purchases per customer. We buy the products for $10.00 and sell them for $24.00, making a profit of $14.00 on each sale. How much is 700 times 14?"

"It totals $9,800.00. So the difference is a profit of $1,050.00."

"That's exactly right, John, and in this example, we actually did better than in reality. I remember that my client told me it came out to plus/minus zero at the end. Isn't zero a wonderful budget to win 700 first-time customers, invite them over to our store, and give them firsthand, live experience of our selection and the quality of our products? Imagine how many tens of thousands of flyers and free vouchers you would have to send out to motivate 700 strangers to show up at your store, many of whom would come to receive their one-time present. But because they wouldn't be from the target group, only a few of them would spend that much extra money on quality food.

"Instead, for years, our butcher has been reaching his exact target group, who is willing to spend a little extra for top quality. How do you like that idea now?"

John was so excited, he could hardly speak. "That is one of the coolest things I ever heard of! It means that if I can identify my target group, I can look for experts who run a different business but serve the same target group. Then I offer them specifically what they could use to bond better with their clients. That way, I am introduced for nearly nothing to a lot of their clients and win them over to become my clients also. The other expert is happy because of the great addition to his customer loyalty program, the clients are happy with their free gift and the introduction to my new business, and I have tons of leads to win over to become clients. Everyone wins in this scenario—that's truly a win-win-win-concept, attracting everybody's heart."

"That is right, John. You got the idea. To make sure that you are not becoming too euphoric, let me add that sometimes you won't have your initial investment paid back completely by additional purchases. But even if you have to invest a few thousand dollars, it's still a steal compared to placing ads, direct mail, free voucher campaigns, and so on. This is your recipe to piggyback networking in a nutshell:

- Be an expert for a certain niche of customers whom you can offer great value.
- Find one or more experts who run a different business but serve the same target group of customers you do.

- Be crystal clear up front which services you can offer your piggyback partner so that he receives really great value for his customer loyalty program.

- Always say that your partner ordered and paid for the gift, so there is no obligation to your partner's customers to pick it up from you.

- Another important point is that in each industry, there are only a handful of experts who are really attractive for long-term cooperation. Win them over before your competition does. We have already seen that in some early bird branches, these techniques have been used for some years. As soon as strong alliances are built, it's very difficult for any outsider to breach them."

The Marketing Master paused and smiled at John, being very well aware that the energy level of his enthusiastic student had gone down a bit. "You look like you are ready for a nap, John—it's time to have fun and let your subconscious work on today's lesson."

John grinned and his eyes were radiating. "No way, I'm not tired at all. I have so many ideas, what to do about word of mouth that I even do not know where to start. Thank you so much for this morning!"

After leaving the Master's office, John ran to the lake. *Gosh, I'm more excited than I was in years. I'll rent a rowboat and get out on the lake as far as I can … that will give me an ever broader perspective!*

After rowing for an hour, John looked back. The town of Starnberg faded away in the distance, and it seemed that he came considerably closer to the mountains at the other end of the lake. *This is the spot to put my ideas down in my diary,* he decided and began writing:

- Word of mouth is the marketing technology of the twenty-first century. With all the new ways people are connected with each other through e-mails, mobile phones, and the Internet, it will become even more effective than in the past.

- Amazon, eBay, Google, YouTube, and a dozen other billion-dollar companies were built through word of mouth. Word of mouth came first, and because they delivered what they had promised, they positioned themselves in our minds and hearts.

- I'll find the customers who are our best communication channels—the ones who already connected their kindergarten friends when they were four and five years old.
- Whenever we do an event again, we carefully integrate our word-of-mouth multipliers.
- We will make a list of the fifty most important opinion leaders in our town and set the goal to win five of them per year as clients.
- We'll inject word-of-mouth marketing into the buying process. We clearly define which buying processes are important enough to invite one or two clients to a phone conference with a prospect. We make a list of our best clients and word-of-mouth multipliers whom we invite to those conferences. We will check every month how many word-of-mouth conferences we did and how successful they were.
- We will develop different emotional stories and test them with the bar stool test.
- And most importantly: We will go for the most interesting piggyback-networking partners before our competition does. We will figure out who are the best experts in other industries are serving our niche of customers. With every potential piggyback-networking partner, we'll do the competitor test: Would it be a real loss if one of our competitors started a networking relationship with the partner we identified first? If yes, we do everything to win this partner within the next six months.

Chapter 4: The Third Heart Magnet: Getting and Staying in Touch

Thursday morning, 6:30 AM—John thoroughly enjoyed his early morning at Lake Starnberg. He was staying at the Forsthaus, one of the nicest hotels on the lake, and had taken a long run to the quaint town of Tutzing and back. Throughout the morning, he marveled about the panoramic vistas of the snow-capped Swiss Alps shimmering brightly on this wonderful spring morning in May. John was sitting on the terrace of the Forsthaus Restaurant, sipping on a great latte macchiato and getting ready to head to the Marketing Master's office. He was more than excited because he already considered the trip to be a great success, just from the knowledge he had gained about expert positioning and power of word of mouth.

But the Master had promised that the magnet of the day—what he called "The mechanics of getting and staying in touch"—would offer John the chance to tap into a powerful new world in marketing that most entrepreneurs were neglecting completely. When John rang the doorbell, the Master smiled broadly, opened the door, greeted him warmly, and said, "What about today? Would you be interested in learning about a lead-generating system that could bring in hundreds or even thousands of qualified business leads each year—and all that for about the cost of producing one little brochure?"

John laughed out loud and replied, "You always have these funny promises where my gut tells me that it's too good to be true. But so far you've delivered every time—so I can't wait; let's go for it!"

1. The Mechanics of Getting in Touch

"John, have you ever heard about LRM or leads relationship management?" the Marketing Master asked with a broad smile.

"No. I haven't, unless it's related to what we call CRM over in the U.S.—customer relationship management. That's a big business and there is a lot of powerful database software designed to attempt to maximize results. Our sales team uses one of these CRM systems, but honestly, we only store the customer's address, birth date, and everything he ever bought from us."

"Well, that's already better than some of my clients do. A lot of them have a database system with the capacity to handle a truckload of information, yet they usually end up only using a briefcase worth of data instead. For those clients who are sophisticated enough to use at least some form of database software, most of the systems are basically useless until a potential customer has already become a client. They do not address at all the steps to take during the critical period of time before they actually become customers, i.e. how to find, manage, and filter leads until you have qualified business prospects that your sales team can turn into first-time customers.

"I have a system that is able to do what I call the GIT Management or ***Getting-in-Touch Management***. Of course you've probably never even heard of this concept because all our industries seem to be missing the boat on this issue. So let me teach you our powerful five-step process to find and qualify leads with better, faster, cheaper, and more emotional bonding than you've ever even dreamed of!

"Remember what I told you on Monday about marketing and its history?" the Master said.

John interrupted him proudly. "Yes, I recall that it comes from the Latin root *'mercatus,'* which means 'doing business in marketplaces.' For approximately three thousand years, only those people who had the need to buy something took action and went to the market to do so. These buyers indicated their interest solely by going to the market. Selling to this self-selected group was easy because the prospects at the market had already determined that they were going to become customers and buy all the veggies that they had run out of at home."

"Wow, what a memory! I've seldom had a student who learned so quickly!" the Marketing Master complimented his student. "John, how would you like it if the good old Roman marketing paradise came back to the business world of today? How would you like to sell your products and services in a worldwide Roman marketplace where millions of interested people would basically raise their hands and indicate their interest all on their own? Where they just showed up on their own initiative and demonstrated proactively that they were interested in buying whatever you were selling?"

"Well, that would be too good to be true, but even with all the optimism in the world, I can't imagine that those times would ever come back," John replied with absolute conviction in his voice.

"You are right! They won't 'come back,' John; they are already here!" the Master exclaimed, and then he paused deliberately and looked at John to see whether he got the message or not.

John was totally confused. "I'm sorry, you lost me," he said. "Are you trying to tell me that the old Roman marketplace where people proactively look for solutions and are actually happy to find out about possible solutions is back?"

"Yes," the Master replied. "It is called the Internet. Every month, hundreds of thousands of people worldwide look up information on a range of diverse topics such as health insurance, pension plans, yoga teachers, and classic cars—and literally every other single market niche that you could imagine. We know that a person might be interested by the mere fact that he is typing a key phrase in an Internet search engine. For example, when someone Googles *pension plan* at one o'clock in the morning, one could conclude that such a potential customer either has a sleeping disorder and/or is extremely interested in the topic he is researching."

John was not impressed. "Yeah, yeah, I know that, but just because millions of people look up some information on the Web doesn't mean that they want to buy anything at all, and it certainly doesn't mean that they want to buy something via the Internet."

"True and not true," the Master replied. "You still can improve on identifying your potential clients. For example, while doing some research for a specific client, I recently discovered that in Germany alone, more than 100,000 people Google *pension plans* every month. Now, perhaps you will speculate that half of those people are students researching material for some project. And maybe you'll tell me that about 90 percent of the remaining 50,000 are really only interested in looking around. And furthermore, probably 90 percent of the 5,000 left are not interested in purchasing anything. They are only looking for free information to help them prepare for their decision about a pension plan. Even so, that still leaves in Germany alone 500 highly interested prospects every single month potentially looking to purchase some sort of product or service for their pension plan. Now if you happened to be an expert in the field of pension plans, wouldn't it be nice if you could offer your services this month to those 500 highly interested people? And wouldn't it be nice if you could do that all year long—and generate 6,000 extremely qualified leads for pension plans each and every year?"

"That would be wonderful," answered John. "But finding these 500 qualified prospects in an ocean also filled with 99,500 spectators sounds even more difficult than finding the proverbial needle in a haystack. It simply sounds impossible!"

The Master smiled and stated, "You still have a major learning curve ahead of you, my friend. Sure, there are millions of entrepreneurs who can tell you why they *can't* find business on the Web. But the world never rewards those who know why things are *not* working. I tell you what: Let me show you how we teach our clients to filter out the qualified 500 buyers from the 99,500 lookers. In return, please tell me about your personal thoughts and beliefs after you are aware the strategy and the tactics. Do we have a deal?"

John nodded in agreement; after all, the Marketing Master had proven him wrong on so many of his prior beliefs. Even so, his feeling that the Internet wouldn't work for him to find clients was very strong, as it was very clear that in the past the Internet had provided very limited results for his business.

"To be successful on the Web, you have to master five simple steps, which most entrepreneurs never get done. Let's have a look at each of them:

a) Generating Traffic

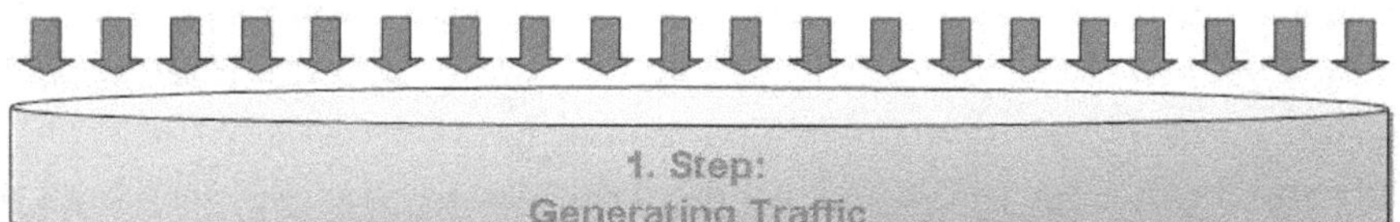

Creating Leads in five steps: Generating Traffic

"A lot of my clients have wonderful home pages. Some of them spent five- or even six-figure budgets to create very impressive and entertaining Web sites. When I ask them how much traffic they generate from their Web sites, I often have to be careful on how I'm to do this because they are so proud of what they created. I oftentimes discover that I have hit a very sore subject for many of them. Most companies these days seem to understand that they need a Web site to serve as their electronic window to the world. What they still do not understand is that ***the most sophisticated and tasteful Web site in the world in and of itself is about as useful as the most wonderfully decorated shopping window in the Sahara Desert.*** If, in front of that window in the desert, there is no street, no parking lot, no bus stop, and no airport, we can safely predict that this store will eventually fail, since traffic is the blood of life for every business.

"So when we start coaching our clients on creating a 'leads pipeline' through the Internet, the first thing we advise them to do to increase their traffic is to consider utilizing search engine optimization techniques as well as Google advertisements. There is plenty of good information out on these topics already, so I will share with you just a couple of short comments:

- It is relatively easy to find a good professional for assistance in search engine optimization. Just Google that term and a few thousand experts will be listed. Since the objective is to improve your placement in search results, the first ten or twenty professionals obviously demonstrate some know-how that their lower-ranked competitors don't have. You should allow approximately three to six months for the SEO specialist to get your Web site into the top ranks.

- If you are not a "techie" yourself, hire a good third-party professional to do the job for you. It's a very specialized field and most likely your limited time will be much better spent elsewhere.
- The advantage of Google advertisements is that you can achieve a top ranking in no time at all—it's solely a matter of cost. In that regard, there are still plenty of niches where you can buy clicks for very little money. Some smaller companies we coach generate more leads than they can handle with budgets of less than $100 per week. As soon as you compete for advertisements on sites with much higher demand, this low-budget advantage starts to disappear because the pay-per-click costs will rise as the popularity of the site on which you are advertising increases. So the first step of creating a leads pipeline is to generate traffic. Yet on this first simple step, it seems that over 90 percent of our clients were already lost at the time we first met with them. And the remaining 10 percent—the ones who actually did get a lot of traffic—usually didn't master the next step.

b) Getting Leads

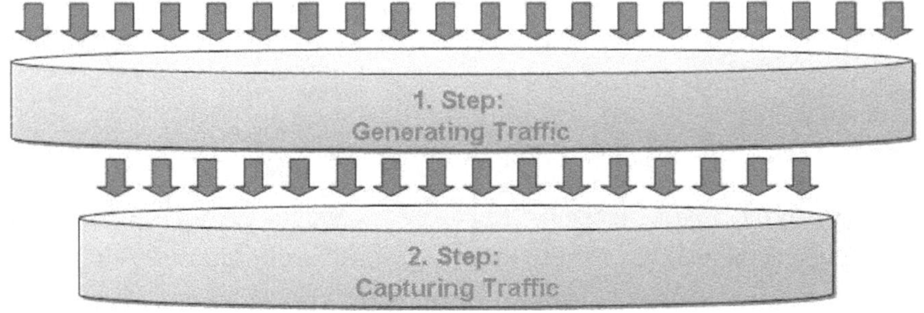

Creating Leads in five steps: Capturing Traffic

"Having a few thousand clicks per week on your Web site may be very nice for your ego, but as long as these potential shoppers disappear without you having a chance to get in touch with them, you really haven't gained very much. So the question becomes how can you motivate, inspire, and invite people to give you their e-mail address so that you can get back to them? Years ago, it may have been enough to offer site visitors a nice newsletter and that seemed enough for people interested in your niche to opt in and provide you with an e-mail address. But as you are no doubt aware, a newsletter alone will rarely do it these days.

"So what we recommend to our clients is to go far beyond this and create what we call *a place of treasures* relating to your relevant subject. For example, assume for the moment that you are one of the leading experts on pension plans. Now imagine that whenever somebody Googled that term, they found your place of treasures showing up as number one in the ranking. Your site would be the most complete and comprehensive Web site on this topic, offering the following items of value:

- A dozen articles from well-known experts on pension plans
- The summary of a book you published on the matter
- Comprehensive checklists like "The Ten Biggest Mistakes to Avoid When Building Your Pension Plan"
- Audio files with tele-seminars of you interviewing leading experts on pension planning
- Video clips from the leading conference on pension planning that you sponsored last year.
- An invitation for a free teleconference on the newest tax laws on pension plans
- Your monthly pension planning newsletter

"Simply think of your place of treasures for pension planners as the most comprehensive Web site around this topic on the Web. Think about it as the *information heaven and paradise* for somebody who needs and wants high-quality information about your area of expertise. Think about that person desperately Googling 'pension planning' at 1:00 AM and finding your lead generator page listed as number one, two, or three on Google. Think about that person being invited by you to get all this information on pension planning with an estimated value of something like $10,000—absolutely free. Whatever your guest clicks on, he will get for free. He simply gives you his name and e-mail address and you send him all the information he is interested in instantly. How cool would that be?

"Now think even further. Let's say your Web page is really intelligent and tracks for you exactly the kind of information each of your guests is interested in. Let's say I was interested in a certain type of pension scheme, like one paying annuities, and I clicked on a relevant link on your site. Your site would automatically send me some info, store the fact that I expressed interest by raising my hand, and a few days later, your auto responder would get back to me asking me how much I liked what you sent to me and whether I had any additional questions you could help me with. In fact, you would be creating a type of Roman marketplace setting with potential clients coming to you to express their interest, but you use technology to follow up and prompt them to continue thinking about your services.

"Two years ago, when we suggested to a client that he should build such a place of treasures Web site, his Web designer charged him somewhere around $2,500, and for a good tracking system maybe another $7,000—which for some smaller clients of ours represented a very substantial part of their marketing budget. Today, you can buy powerful software tools that help you build such a place of treasures Web site in less than two hours. These tools include a database for leads, all the marketing tracking, auto responders, and all landing page and sales letter generators you ever need. And the best thing about all that is that today these tools cost you less than $40.00 a month!"

John began to see the possibilities, but he wasn't completely convinced yet. "I can see that you can build a powerful Web site to invite people to leave their names and e-mail addresses—so I can see how to generate tons of leads. But in my experience, most Web surfers are only interested in free information. So I'm still not convinced that you can generate highly interested buyers this way."

"You are perfectly right, John." The Master nodded in complete agreement. "In assuming that the average quality of leads generated this way is less than to be desired. That's the reason why we created the next three filters to improve further the quality of your leads. And my promise to you is that everybody who is still with you in phase five is a highly qualified hot prospect. Let's continue to the next filter."

c) The Leads Qualification

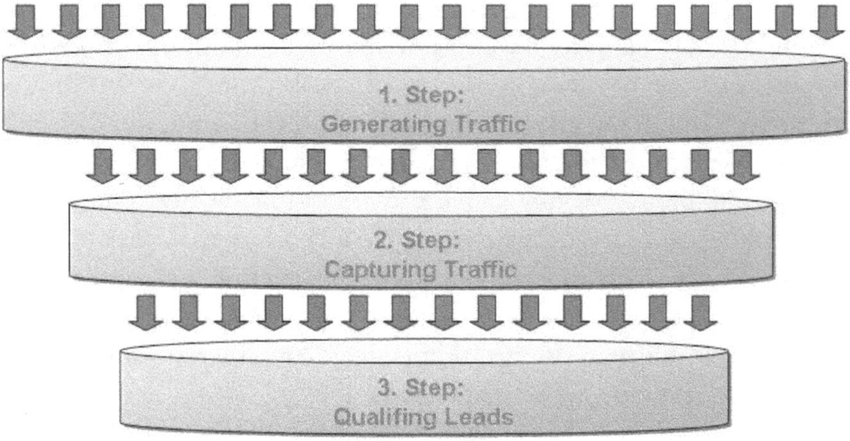

1. Step:
Generating Traffic

2. Step:
Capturing Traffic

3. Step:
Qualifing Leads

Creating Leads in five steps: Leads Qualification

"Because there are so many people on the Web searching only for free information, we found it extremely helpful to identify those people who are truly interested in more than just looking and who are willing to act on that interest—even if it only takes them a minute to do so. Does that make sense?"

"Yes, that makes a lot of sense," John agreed.

The Master continued. "To invite people to raise their arm again and document their interest in, let's say, pension planning, our auto responder sends them a little note a few days after they received the information they requested. It could read something like this:

Hello Bill,

Thank you very much for your interest in pension planning. We hope that the information we sent to you helped you to answer all of your questions. Yesterday, I was thinking about your request again, and I found a brand-new article on pension planning which heretofore has not yet been published on our Web site. So I'm sending you this article, hoping that you will enjoy it as much as we did when it comes to finding the newest tax information on pension plans. By the way, Bill, I wanted to let you know that a few colleagues of mine and I are now working on compiling the most comprehensive documentation on pension plans anybody has ever done in Germany. We are working on the final chapter as we speak and we believe this work will answer virtually all of the burning questions our clients have around pension plans.

Actually, to make sure our work addresses all of our clients' questions, we are asking them to share their most important questions with us. We would greatly appreciate it if you would share with us your most interesting question on pension plans. Just click on the link below and type your question into the opening window. In return for your support on this issue, we would like to send you our 250-page document on pension plans—co-authored by eight of the most well-known experts in this field. This is valued at $249—completely free of charge.

Just give us three to four weeks to finish the last chapter and it will be yours as soon as it is complete!

Thanks for all of your support and input and we are looking forward to receiving your question as soon as possible. Have a great day!

Sincerely yours,

XYZ

"Do you see what we are doing here, John? Most of the information junkies who only are interested in the free stuff won't bother to take the time to send you the questions they are really interested in. And by the way, we do not always offer a reward for sending in questions. In those cases, the fact that somebody responds is even greater proof of his genuine interest.

"As an aside, we collect all the questions in another wonderful little piece of software called the 'ask database.' Our clients invest less than $30 a month for it and do all their marketing research with clients and prospects for less than $400 a year! I will come back to this later when we talk about Socratic marketing. For now it is only important to remember that our clients—after collecting a few hundred questions—will get a neat little list from that software giving them the prospective clients' top ten hottest questions on pension planning. This will enable them to proceed to step number four."

d. Bonding with your leads and touching your prospects' hearts

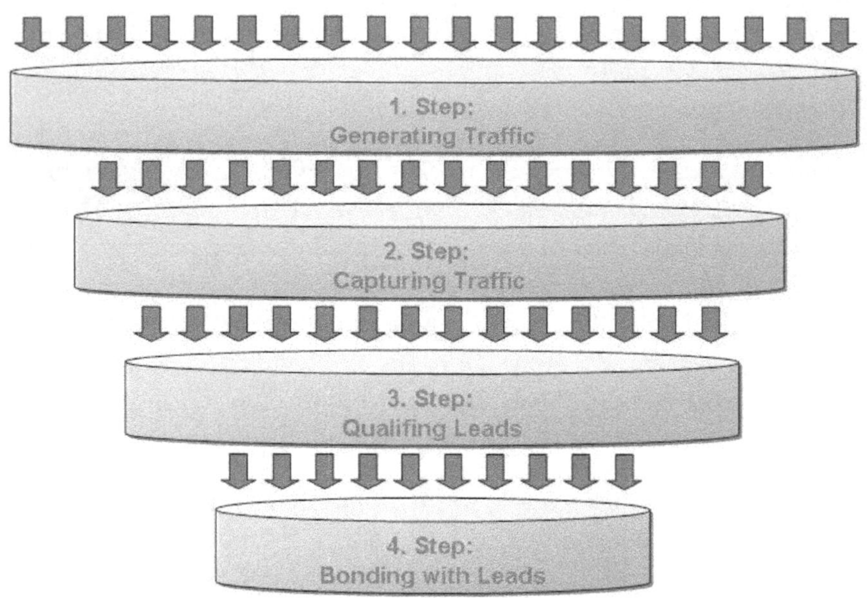

Creating Leads in five steps: Bonding with Leads

"What we typically do at this point is to invite the prospects who took the time to give us their most important questions to attend a free tele-seminar intended to address each of those questions. May I ask, John, are you already familiar using tele-seminars in your industry?"

John responded. "I've heard about them but I have never participated in one. Is that a kind of telephone conference where the participants basically listen to a coach of some sort giving a seminar?"

"In a way, I suppose yes, but it is actually much more than that. We now have a software package that allows your participants to go to a Web site where they can look at your computer screen concurrent with the tele-conference so that they will be able to:

- View your PowerPoint presentation.
- See any other file from your desktop you want to show during the conference, such as a letter from your clients or certain Excel spreadsheets; if desired, you will be able to change the displayed files while you discuss them with your participants.

- Surf the Net to access any other Web site you may direct them to—for example, you may want to take them to your online store and explain some of your products, or direct them to a Web site with a specialized pension plan calculator.
- Observe your use of very specialized and powerful flipchart software from Israel that allows you to draw or write virtually anything on a piece of paper and have it displayed on your (and their) computer screen so that you can demonstrate to them visually as if they were sitting next you.

"Now, that's pretty cool, isn't it?"

"That's really special. I'm very impressed!" John replied. "That would open the ability for me to utilize completely new approaches to deliver value to my clients by explaining complex things in simpler ways so everybody can understand."

"That's true," said the Master, "and if you want to do even better than that, you can send all your participants relevant documentation of your seminar with one simple click of the mouse. The computer memorizes which slides and files you showed them and will send them to your clients in exactly the same order."

"Wow, that is even cooler than what I thought was possible!" John exclaimed excitedly, as the Master added quickly: "Oh, it's a wonderful technology, but before we get too excited exploring all of the possibilities it opens up for your communication with clients and prospects, please allow me to show you how we use it to find the best-qualified prospects the Internet has to offer. Remember Bill, the guy who sent us his top-priority question relating to pension plans? After he sends us his question, we will get back to him with an invitation to a tele-seminar that addresses precisely his question, as well as the top-priority questions of others in a similar situation. To give you an idea, the invitation could look like this:

Dear Bill,

Thank you so much for sharing your most important question on pension planning with us. We really appreciate it and will address your question in our documentation on pension plans that we'll send to you as promised in a few weeks.

Actually, your question seems to be related to one of the real hot topics when it comes to pension plans. It ranks among the top three on your list of the hottest topics. Indeed, several of our other clients actually called our office and asked us to answer their questions immediately. Given the urgency of their situations, we found that many of them didn't want to even wait until our documentation is complete to have their question addressed. To accommodate these requests, we have decided to offer a telephone conference addressing the seven hottest questions we received from our clients next Monday. The topics are:

- *A*
- *B*

Our coaching session will take place via teleconference and will last approximately sixty to ninety minutes. It will be accompanied by a simultaneous presentation on the Internet and we hope that you will be able to be online so that you can follow our documentation there. In addition to the presentation, we will have a live discussion of your question and the questions of others to the extent that they are not adequately covered by the presentation. Our phone conference system can host 100 participants, and we have already had 87 of our customers sign up immediately for the conference. This is a conference that we offer only to our best customers at the very special price of $99, but Bill, because your question is one of the central parts of the conference and you were kind enough to help us out with your input, we would like to invite you as our very special VIP guest to attend the meeting completely free of charge.

Please click the link below as soon as possible so that you can reserve your space before our conference sells out. Simply put in your name and the phone number where you want our system to call you on Monday night at precisely 6:00 PM.

We are very much looking forward to meeting you on the tele-seminar on Monday and to addressing everything you would like to know about pension plans!

Warmest regards,

XYZ

"Wow, that's really cool," John marveled. "If I were Bill and you invited me at no charge to attend a phone conference that exactly addressed my top-priority question as well as other similar issues, I think I would go for it."

"Exactly," the Master agreed. "Not all prospects who have sent in a question will join the conference, but the ones who really raised their hand again to indicate their interest in pension planning will. And it's time for the final one of the five steps.

e) The Irresistible Offer

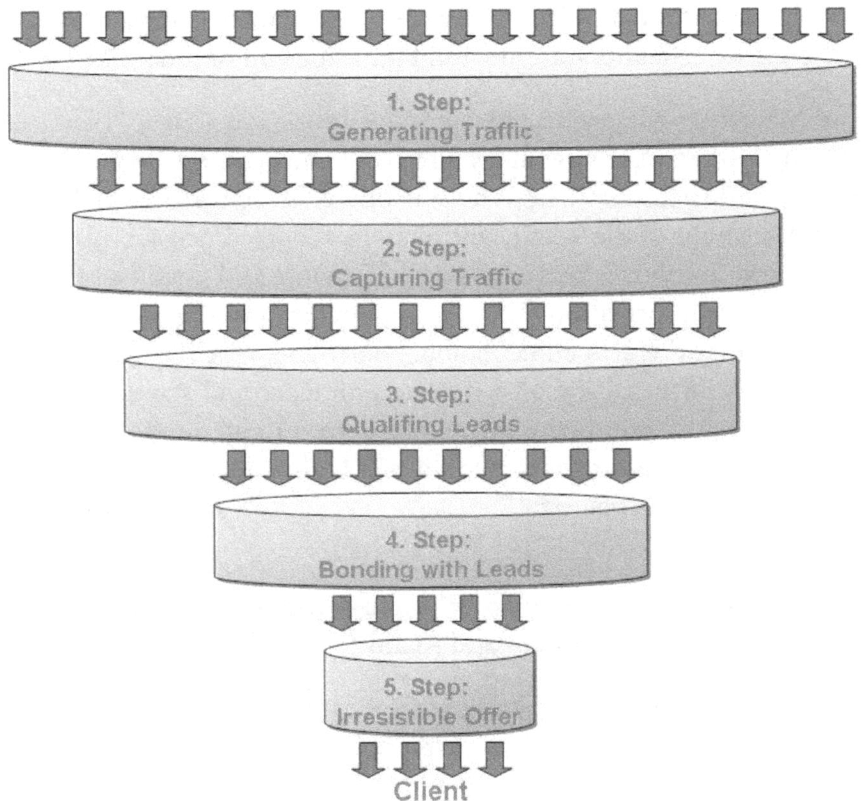

Creating Leads in five steps: The Irresistible Offer

"The feedback we've gotten from our clients when one qualifies leads through a tele-conference is that prospects who participated in such conferences are at least three times more likely to become clients than prospects generated by any other method. Obviously, a potential client will enjoy the experience of participating in a live dialogue and having the opportunity to ask questions and receive answers to his questions as well as other valuable information. This approach to prospecting is, not surprisingly, a much more powerful tool to entice customers to do business with you than your everyday flyer with a description of your products and services. To continue the progress of reeling in that customer, we recommend to our clients to present yet another special offer to their prospects during the phone conference. Something along the lines of, "We really appreciate that you spent so much time with us today. If you want to find out even more on pension plans, we have a very special offer that we are presenting only to the participants of this tele-conference and that is only valid until the end of today …"

The Marketing Master paused, smiled at John, and stated, "Now, tell me, in this last case, how many times did the prospect have to show and prove his interest before he was offered a personal consultation with a member of the sales team? First, he Googled pension planning on his own initiative. Second, he gave his name and e-mail address to get some free information. Third, he sent in his hottest question on the topic to support this documentation. Fourth, he signed up for the tele-conference. Fifth, he attended the teleconference and stayed until the end. And sixth, after being invited, he agreed to an appointment for *information-for-free-surfers* to a few dozen highly qualified prospects—and yes, that's very powerful."

2. The Mechanics of Staying in Touch—and Reaching your Customer's Heart Again and Again

"What is the easiest way to generate more sales?" the Marketing Master asked John, to address the next chapter of their coaching.

"In my experience, it is a lot easier to sell more to existing customers than to find new ones," John replied.

The Master nodded in agreement. "So tell me what you do to take care of your relationship with existing customers."

"Well, we send them a birthday card, a Christmas card, and invite them twice a year to our open house—and of course, we send them our e-mail newsletter," John said, feeling pretty good that he could come up with so many good-sounding actions.

"Well, honestly," the Master responded as he looked directly into John's eyes, "do you believe that what you're doing is effective to touch your customer emotionally and build a long-lasting bond between you and him, ideally a lifelong relationship? And do you think you're doing an outstanding job of preparing him for cross selling?" the Master asked, raising his eyebrows.

John shook his head and the Master continued. "Please, explain to me why you—like most entrepreneurs—agree that taking care of your existing clients is the easiest way to new business, yet when it comes to acting on that insight, you really don't follow through."

John shrugged his shoulders. "I really don't know. I think it is that we are so overwhelmed with work and I'm really not that disciplined. So, I guess in some ways, it's a lack of motivation."

The Marketing Master smiled at John and said, "During the first years of my career, I thought the same way you did. And because I trained our German national Olympic coaches for years on motivating their athletes for peak performances, I came up with a top-of-the-line, highly advanced motivation concept for salespeople to follow through at customer relationship management. And do you know what?"

"I have no idea," John muttered.

The Master continued,. "It was a complete disaster. It worked for four weeks, but after that, everything was back to where it had started, with the salespeople going back to hunting for new clients and leaving the existing customers on the back burner once again.

"My breakthrough in that area came when I remembered what I leaned from Edward W. Deming, the father of modern quality management. As you may recall from our discussion on Monday, he told us that 94 percent of all failures are system failures as opposed to individual ones. Taking that insight into account and analyzing how customer relationship management is done in small and medium-sized companies, I immediately found two culprits: first, most companies simply do not have an effective contact management system in place, and second, the one they use is more often than not far away from touching the customer emotionally. To put it very plainly: *When you start your computer in the office on Monday morning and the first thing you get is anything other than a list of those clients you have to contact this week, chances are that the tyranny of the most urgent issues will win again this week over the high, but less urgent, priority of strengthening your relationship with existing customers!*

"By the way, John, have you ever thought about the fact that each quarter of a year has thirteen weeks and that the English alphabet has twenty-six letters, and that both of those are multiples of thirteen? Even the slowest thinker must figure out that that can't be an accident and has to be God's special gift to entrepreneurs," the Marketing Master said with a huge grin.

"Well, then I must be slower than the slowest thinker. Sure, thirteen times two is twenty-six. But how can that help me with my systematic contact management with my customers?" John replied, a little confused.

"Well, it will allow you to contact all your clients whose names start with A and B in the first week of a quarter, the ones with C and D in the next week, and so on until you contact Y and Z in week thirteen. As simple as it may look, this little trick is a huge organizational help to many of my clients. If, for example, you have a total of 400 clients and you divide them into 13 groups of approximately 30 or so, you leave yourself a very manageable list of customers to contact every week. And if the computer of your marketing assistant starts every Monday by printing out the list of customers to be contacted this week, the chances that you achieve this specific goal will increase dramatically.

"Now, do we have a second for some fun?" the Master asked John with a big grin.

"Of course we do," John replied, thinking that he never thought of Germans as being particularly funny.

The Master still had a huge grin on his face and said, "Believe it or not, when I explained that alphabetical organizational tool to a big group of entrepreneurs a few weeks ago, one participant objected and stated, 'I like that idea a lot! But it wouldn't work for me that well, because. For example, the week with S and T will have a lot more customers than week thirteen with Y and Z.' So I said to him, 'That's exactly right, but knowing that, couldn't you simply adjust the group size in a way that you have every week roughly the same number of customers to touch base with?' He looked at me in complete disbelief and said, 'Oh, I didn't think this was allowed with your method.'"

John laughed out loud. He had heard that Germans are very orderly people. But that they could be that inflexible … unbelievable!

The Master added, "So don't take that advice verbatim. Take up the idea behind it and clearly define the clients to be contacted each week as your contact management homework. Maybe you want to touch base with your most important customers twice in a quarter, with your next tier of B clients once a quarter, and with your C clients every other quarter.

"The next important point is to define every customer contact ahead of time for the whole year. So if you want to send all your clients a Happy New Year greeting card, write the card when you do your marketing plan. In the event that you want to call them six weeks later with a special spring offer, write the outline for the phone call in advance. Remember, the hallmark of a powerful contact-management system is that you define every step and every contact in a way that for the rest of the year there is no more planning required. This minimizes the potential for interference with the smooth execution of the plan.

"One other important advice for your contact-management system is this: Avoid corporate speak at all costs!"

"What do you mean by corporate speak?" asked a perplexed John.

"Well, for example, think of your phone company. Once in a while, do you get a letter from AT&T or Sprint or maybe your local electricity company or any other big corporation?"

"Of course I do," John replied.

"Well, with very few exceptions," the Master continued, "do you think of these letters as personal messages to you, or do they feel like advertisements going out to millions of customers?"

"They aren't personal, and I think you can't be personal when you write to millions of customers!" John proclaimed.

"I completely disagree," the Master stated firmly. "One of my clients in Germany is Yello, an electric utility company with more than 800,000 customers. They are the one and only company in their industry who sends a handwritten birthday card to each customer each year. They bought a special software package with computerized 'handwriting' that you cannot distinguish from a real person's handwriting. They sign it with the name of one of their employees in the customer service department. Every week, they get dozens of handwritten letters, often even two-page letters, from people who were positively surprised that Yello was thoughtful enough to think of them on their birthday. There is a wall in their customer department thirty feet wide and ten feet high covered with response letters written by happy clients.

"So what I'm suggesting here, especially if you are not a corporate giant, is this: Be as personal as you can be when writing to your clients. Write as if you wrote to your best friend. Start with things like, 'I'm sitting on my balcony enjoying this nice summer evening and just started thinking about you …' We tested it and found that customers love this personal touch. *We get five to thirty times more feedback—even when we didn't ask for it—from 'personal' letters than from corporate speak!"*

John was taking notes as fast as he could. The Master looked on John's notepad and read:

- Define A, B, and C clients.
- Contact A clients four times a year, B clients twice, and C clients once.
- Define for each week (from 1 to 52) exactly which clients are contacted in those weeks.
- Write all letters in advance. If the contact is to be made via a phone call, outline its content in a draft that is specific enough that your assistant can execute it.
- Write personally; use the huge advantage of 'personal touch' that small and medium companies have over big corporations.

- Don't worry about spontaneity. When the system is in place, you always can initiate additional activities spontaneously, addressing new issues that come up over the course of the year.
- The contact system is your security policy that your bond with the client will never stop.

"That's great," the Master complimented John. "You've really got it. There is only one last important point to add: I know a lot of companies that only write to their clients when they are offering another buying opportunity. That way they are communicating loud and clear that their customer only matters when it comes to business. Think about a friend who calls you three times a year and every time he calls you, he either wants to borrow your car or is looking for a babysitter. Even if you started out with a great friendship, chances are that his way of functionalizing the friendship will damage it in the long run. There is a German proverb that shows the way. 'Small presents preserve the relationship.' So think about it: What are little presents of your time, energy, or know-how that you could offer to your clients only with the purpose of showing your appreciation for your clients and their business? If you find a way of touching their hearts with little gifts of appreciation a few times a year, chances are that they perceive your cross-selling invitations with an open mind too. Does that make any sense?"

"Of course it does," John answered with a loud sigh, thinking about all the things coming to his mind he could do to improve his business. "That's great! Then let's have a break before we take a look on how to work with the next powerful tool."

3. Touching the Customer's Heart with Every Experience: The Customer Experience Pipeline

"We've already talked about the great progress companies have made with Total Quality Management—TQM—over the last thirty years. Basically every different type of production process you can imagine was totally taken apart and analyzed down to the last screw. The Japanese model of *kaisen*—the process of constant and never ending improvement—seems to have been implemented everywhere in the United States and in Europe with regard to production issues."

The Master paused for a moment to emphasize his next statement. "So in the engineering of production processes, many companies have achieved world-class standards. But what blows my mind is this: If you look at the same company to analyze what they've done to improve customer service over the last thirty years—you'll very often find that they've done absolutely nothing. Many of them don't even know the chronology of customer service experience in their own company!"

"What do you mean by *chronology of customer service experience?"* John asked quickly, as he sensed that the Master was truly irritated by that lack of professionalism of companies in this regard.

"Let me give you an example," the Master began to explain. "Two years ago, I was hired by a five-star Austrian hotel to install and apply a service improvement process. They already had a very good marketing concept in place and were, in fact, very sought after by customers for conferences as well as for upscale wellness vacations.

"When I arrived at the hotel that evening at around 11:00 PM, they must have been sold out completely. It was impossible to find a space for my car in the parking lot and I had to leave the property to park outside, about a hundred yards away in a meadow. When I arrived at the reception desk, the owner was just talking to one of his front desk clerks. I knew him from a previous seminar, and he greeted me warmly. I asked him if he had five minutes to discuss starting a little 'client experience pipeline.' He grinned and stated that he didn't have any idea what I was talking about but that it sounded interesting. I told him that I would pick him up with my car in one minute, which I did. Then I told him that he needed to step into the shoes of his customers and observe their experience as they arrived at his hotel. So I drove up to the reception area once again, could not find a parking spot in the main lot, searched through the other two parking lots on the property, left the property, and finally parked in the meadow again. We walked back through the dirt—it was raining a little bit by now—and I told him: 'That's the first impression from a guest's point of view when arriving at night at your hotel,' to which he responded, 'I knew that it was bad. But having my reserved spot in the garage, I had no idea it could be that bad.'

"So when I talk about analyzing a customer's experience pipeline, I suggest the following: First of all, *list all the experiences a customer will have with your company in chronological order.* For example, if the customer usually talks with the telephone receptionist first, then that is his first experience. If he then needs to wait three minutes to be connected to the service department, then this is his second experience. In the event he finds himself connected to the wrong department, this is experience number three. The service representative to whom he ultimately speaks may at that point listen to your customer's complaint, and at that point might add, 'I'm sorry, but it is not my fault', which then would become experience number four.

"My message to you is this: During all phases that your customer comes in touch with your company, you are producing an emotional experience for your customer at that moment. My suggestion is that you look at each of those experience-producing phases as one part of your customer's experience production process. That process is happening in your customer's mind, and whether you intend it or not, it is orchestrated by the way you conduct each interaction with him. Then you can take all your *kaizen* know-how from TQM to improve each of these phases in a step-by-step manner, taking all necessary actions to fine tune your service system and the standards of service behavior delivered by your employees to make sure that you touch your customer emotionally. And because different folks enjoy different strokes, the art as well as the fun in that process are to orchestrate many different signals to increase the chance of really reaching out to every client. Think about the check-in at a hotel. Some guests may enjoy having an employee offer to park their car, others may like a welcome drink, or finding fresh flowers or a fruit basket in their room—chances are, when you offer all of that, you'll have included at least one thing that they really like. Remember the first stages of a love relationship. If you don't know whether your love prefers flowers, a short good-night phone call, or an enthusiastic text message first thing in the morning—chances are you offer all of it, don't you?

"To finish my example with the Austrian five-star hotel, the next day, I decided to take all of the service employees of the hotel on a tour in an attempt to get them to view everything from a guest's perspective.

For example, when we were heading to their new wellness area—a $2 million spa they had just built—we ended up walking through a hallway in the basement. In front of the entrance door, there were three trolleys packed with dirty laundry. Everybody was passing them by without a word of explanation. So I asked: 'Why is this dirty laundry parked just in front of the spa entrance?' They all froze until one employee finally said, 'Behind you is the door through which the laundry company can access the facility with a truck. So it's always parked here. Until now, it had never been a problem, because our guests never came to the basement. But with the new spa entrance here, I suppose … well, yes, we understand your point.'"

John was busy again taking notes, and the Marketing Master read what he had written while glancing over his shoulder:

- TQM is as important in service processes as it is for production processes.
- In the production world, everybody uses TQM. When it comes to service, however, many companies don't, and this gives us an opportunity to outperform the competition.
- We will list all possible situations where a customer comes in touch with our company and interacts with us.
- We will list these experiences in chronological order.
- We will look at each experience separately and ask ourselves what we can do to improve the systems involved and the standards of employee behavior.
- We will work on these service processes step by step with our *kaizen* philosophy: constant and never-ending improvement.

The Master smiled at John; he knew when he had found an excellent student! So he asked John, "Have you ever read the works of Peter Drucker, the dean of modern management?"

"Of course I have," John answered. "I think he has been the most brilliant thinker on entrepreneurship and management in the last few decades!"

"I think so too," the Master agreed. "So do you know his most famous quote on marketing and innovation?"

"Yes I do," John smiled; he was very proud of himself. "It is: 'there are only two functions of entrepreneurship: Marketing and innovation—everything else is cost.'"

"That's exactly right!" the Master proclaimed, at this point very impressed with John. "So let's think about how we can use marketing for our innovation processes. You will see, the more you get the concepts of marketing and innovation combined into one synergistic process, the faster and more profitably your company will grow."

4. Touching Your Customer's Heart through Offering What He Wants and Likes Most: Socratic Marketing

"What do you know about Socrates?" the Marketing Master finally asked, coming back to his question from Monday.

"That's the guy who never wrote anything down. Everything we know about him we know from his student Plato, who wrote down some of the marvelous dialogues between Socrates and his disciples."

"True," the Master agreed, "Socrates was the master of generating thought by asking questions. He believed that all the answers were already in the minds of his students and that they only needed the right questions to activate that wisdom. By the way, the word *education* stems from the origins of the Socratic philosophy and originally meant *to draw forward*."

John interrupted the Master to ask a question. "Are you saying that 'education' was originally the process of teachers enticing the right answers from their students by activating their inherent wisdom through questions? If so, then the American educational system has this whole process totally turned upside down. Many of our teachers seem to believe that their students don't know anything about the material, so they pretty much have to tell them everything."

"Same here in Germany," replied the Master. "But what is even worse is that our marketing people are just as short-sighted as our teachers are. Too often they operate on the assumption that they have all of the answers to their clients' needs, and all they teach them is advertising. You will be able to bypass most of your competition if you can understand what Socrates already understood 2,000 years ago: Your clients already have the answers! For example, if you run a company that offers a variety of seminars, why bother every year to figure out which hottest topics will attract your clients? Why not simply ask them? Do an e-mail survey using the ask database, offer some attractive rewards for the first fifty clients responding, and in a couple of days, you may have 100, 200, or more replies out of a list of 1,000 clients. All you have to do is ask a few questions about hot marketing topics, entice them to indicate what is most interesting to them, and you take all the guesswork out of your marketing for the rest of your life! Would that be cool or would that be cool?"

"That would be super cool!" John agreed. "Do you really think your customers will answer those surveys? Maybe the first time they would, but after that, I would think they will get really tired being used as your marketing focus team."

"Are you guessing or do you know that for sure?" the Master wanted to know. He smiled at John with the knowledge that he had this natural habit of always wanting to look at the risks first as opposed to at the rewards.

"Oh, that is only a guess," John mused. "But if I were asked by my suppliers a couple of times a year about input for their product improvement, I wouldn't necessarily see what was in it for me!"

"Great point, John," commended the Master. "You are absolutely right. When you ask your clients to help you with your survey, you have to first find a convincing answer to the question that is in each of their heads, namely, 'Dude, what's in it for me?'

"Actually, we have found that there are basically two kinds of clients: some are reward-oriented while others are more communication-oriented. Accordingly, the appropriate approach is to:

- Tell both groups why their feedback is extremely important.

- Tell both groups how much you appreciate the fact that they take the time to read your letter and how much you value it when they take five to seven minutes of their time to answer.
- Tell them the truth about how much time is needed to answer the questions–that it usually shouldn't be more than ten minutes.
- Offer some interesting prizes to the reward-oriented groups—perhaps weekend vacations for two people in a five-star hotel or maybe tickets to attend a seminar valued at $ 1,000 or more. Interestingly enough, chances are there are many clients out there who would like an even deeper bonding with you. You can find out which ones by sending and explaining to them the results of the survey. Clients who subsequently write back to you are much more interested in the relationship-building than in material rewards. Taking this valuable information one step further, some word-of-mouth research companies use that phenomenon even more and only reward their partners for their input with detailed results and explanations, thereby creating independent contractors who work with them for many years whereby the sole reward is being among the first to have access to the new information."

The Master paused to check his watch. "John, I'm sorry, I'm having a lunch appointment in fifteen minutes. Do you have any questions?"

"Only one. What we covered this morning seems to me more a company building program for a year or two then a four-week project. Am I too pessimistic or is that true?"

The Master was astonished and really impressed. "John, you are outstanding! When I present the getting-in-touch systems, my clients usually estimate that they can introduce these programs in four to eight weeks and really make them work smoothly. Nothing could be further from the truth! Your estimate is very correct. To build a lead-generating pipeline and make your client contact management really run smoothly and effectively, one year is a very fair guess when you do it right!"

"Well, then I'm on the right track," John smiled. "I'll visit my Italian place on the lake, get two or three lattes, and write down my action list." Daydreaming vividly about his company being the leader in utilizing getting-in-touch systems, John put those ideas in his diary:

- In a year from now, we will have another Web site with tons of high-quality information.
- We will appear in the first ten listings on Google.
- We will buy the right Google advertisements so that we can easily be found by everybody who is researching our products.
- We will offer articles, podcasts, short video summaries, checklists for people describing how they can find the right expert, and our benefit-loaded newsletter.
- We will start a dialogue with these prospects.
- The ones who write back are our highly interested leads.
- We will further qualify them with questions about their needs.
- We will invite them to our service tele-conferences. This way, they will get in touch with our service people hosting the calls. We will build a relationship and invite them with irresistible offers.
- We will develop a contact management system.
- "Little presents preserve the relationship." Therefore, we develop three little heart-touching presents for our clients every year.
- We will contact them more often to touch their heart than to send them additional offers.
- We will develop an experience pipeline. We list all the situations where a customer can be in contact with our company. We rate the experience he has now with us on a scale of one to ten. Every time we evaluate the present situation with less than an eight, we design an alternative that rates at least an eight.

- Twice a year, we invite half of our clients to ask detailed questions about products and services we are or should be developing. That way we question each customer only once a year. We will figure out what features and benefits they will like best about new products we are developing. And then we develop exactly what the clients want—yes, we go for the Socratic way!

Chapter 5: The Fourth Heart Magnet: Humanics or how to win over your team with a five-star service philosophy and have them look forward to changing company processes

Friday morning, 10:15 AM—John arrived fifteen minutes late at the Marketing Master's office. The intensive learning of the last few days had begun to take its toll. He had been brainstorming about many ideas until well after midnight, and this morning, he slept through his alarm, not waking until after 9:00 AM.

As always, the Marketing Master opened the door himself and greeted John cordially with a huge smile. "You look like somebody who's been working hard the last few nights." He immediately zoned in on John's reduced energy level. "Why don't we take it easy today? I promise that we'll only talk about important, fun stuff, and I guarantee you that even with the most sophisticated note-taking, you will write down a maximum of six bullet points all day. Do we have a deal?" he asked in a manner that radiated so much energy that John's spirit lifted immediately.

Smiling, John replied, "You really have a way of waking people up with big promises!"

"That's true," the Master replied. **"If you can't deliver the *why* first, most people don't even bother to be interested in the *what* and *how*!"**

John thought a moment about this quote and then started to write it down.

"I have to be careful what I tell you," the Master grinned. "That was a bonus point. It is not part of the six bullet points I was thinking about. Let's get started with our topic for the day: Humanics, with the operative question focused on how to build a team in a way that it magnetically attracts customers and touches their hearts."

1. Implementing a Five-star Service Philosophy

"John, have you ever flown on Singapore Airlines?"

"Yes, they are my favorite airline. Whenever I had to fly to the Far East for my former employer and I could find a way to fly with Singapore, I would. Their flight attendants have really mastered the art of making every guest feel like royalty."

"Well, then we agree about their service, and their example certainly proves that your service team has a huge influence on whether or not your clients feel dramatically drawn to your company, wouldn't you agree?"

"Sure, I agree. The need for outstanding service is a no-brainer, but in reality, there are very few companies capable of actually achieving five-star customer service. It must be difficult to get employees to embrace such a concept."

"Are we looking for problems here or solutions?" the Master asked with a knowing smile.

"I'd definitely prefer to find solutions," John confirmed. "But in my view, looking for effective solutions requires looking at the difficulties many companies have implementing them, and why so many of them never achieve what they set out to do when it comes to customer service," John said, defending his perspective.

"We differ in this regard, John, because I prefer working with companies and entrepreneurs who think that it is easy to achieve brilliant service, and who ultimately demonstrate an outstanding service level for every customer at every opportunity," the Master replied. "**Knowing why something is difficult is actually one of the perceptual handicaps in figuring out how easy things can be.** *Be careful with 'why' questions when it comes to finding solutions*—they often hide the fresh perspective that offers the solution.

"Let's make things easy and have a look at five-star-rated hotels all over the world. With very few exceptions, they all deliver five-star service. Let's say out of a hundred five-star hotels, ninety-five deliver exceptional service. This should prove that it shouldn't be that hard to do. All you have to do is copy what the successful hotels are doing.

"Another interesting fact is that you can find five-star service in hotels in virtually every corner of the world. This obviously helps prove that you can train people from literally every culture to deliver the same level of service.

"There is a third point: the fifteen-year-old elevator operator in a five-star hotel, new to his job, typically has the same genuine friendliness and generous smile as every other employee who has been working there for decades and treats every guest as a VIP. Are you with me so far?"

"Yes, I am completely with you," John answered, already mesmerized with the perspective the Master was teaching him.

"Now tell me," asked the Master, "what conclusions can we draw about the culture in five-star service hotels?"

John smiled and said, "Number one: If a fifteen-year-old, low-paid elevator operator can learn to deliver five-star service during the very first days and weeks he is on the job, then anyone can learn the same in no time at all.

"Number two: Because five-star hotels exist in every culture, people from every culture can be trained to achieve these standards. So, the real question is, *What do five-star hotels know about training and developing a culture for five-star service that most other companies miss?*"

The Master smiled, truly enjoying John's wit and his precise analysis. "That was great, John. You just identified the two most negative sets of beliefs of those cultures. The first mental block you eliminated is the belief that it takes highly qualified and highly paid individuals with years of training to enable people to deliver outstanding service. The example of the elevator operator shows us that *under the right circumstances,* anyone can and will learn what has to be learned, in terms of attitude and behavior, in order to be a service star in a matter of weeks.

"The second limiting belief you identified is the assumption that people of certain cultures will never be able to deliver great service. For example, many airlines believe that Singapore Airlines has better service because their people are raised in a 500-year-old Samurai tradition, supposedly giving them a huge advantage when it comes to discipline and delivering service.

"Similarly, years ago, many American car manufacturers mistakenly believed that their Japanese competitors had a huge advantage in delivering high-quality cars due to the dedication of their workers. They assumed that the dedication to high quality was the result of the values of the Samurai tradition having been imprinted on them for centuries. Yet, when Toyota finally built their first plant in America and trained their American workers to achieve the same quality standards they had in Japan after a mere six months, the belief of the cultural advantage was finally destroyed and the great excuse of a cultural handicap was eliminated forever."

"I agree," John said, "but now that we know that everybody can learn it in weeks and that cultural traditions are neither an advantage nor an excuse, the question still remains: How does a five-star hotel teach an elevator operator to deliver five-star service in a matter of weeks? What do they know about service development that so many other companies are obviously missing?"

The Marketing Master appreciated John's eagerness and desire. "When you are in a hurry, walk slowly. It saves you time! There are dozens of self-proclaimed 'experts' who can teach you about the differences between the service training programs of five-star hotels compared to those of two- or three-star hotels. But looking at the differences in training behavior, they've already missed the boat. Do you have any idea which boat I'm talking about?

"It is this:

- In every first-class hotel, five-star service is **not optional**. It is not only nice to have or even extremely important, it is a prerequisite for doing business—**it is a must!**
- In the best service companies in the world, i.e., the Ritz Carlton, a five-star service culture is not a means to an end. Rather, it is an end value in itself as to how to do business!"

There was a long pause; John obviously needed some time to digest what he had just heard. "When I look at myself," he finally said, "I can see that all the things in my mind that I consider to be a **'must,'** such as brushing my teeth, having breakfast, and going jogging in the morning, simply get done. But many of the things I tell myself I **should** do, such as cleaning my desk or shopping for groceries, I usually don't seem to get around to." With a grin, he added, "Until our refrigerator is so empty that it becomes a must to do the shopping. Then I'll get it done easily!"

"You got it," the Master agreed. "That's precisely the first crucial point that many leaders and managers are missing. As long as the development of a five-star service culture isn't a must, or, shall we say as the Romans did, a *'conditio sine qua non'* it is simply not going to happen.

"So the attitude and commitment of the management becomes the most crucial step. When Toyota came to America, in the minds of Toyota managers, the alternative of not delivering top quality was not even considered to be an option. At that time, all of the American car manufacturers were 'wishing' and 'hoping' and working for better quality. But after Toyota began to deliver top quality in the United States, their competitors essentially noticed their own empty refrigerators and concluded that Total Quality Management became a must over here as well.

"This change in attitude is the first major step, but after it is accomplished, the training of service behavior becomes quite easy. If one approaches it in the same manner as the five-star hotels do, which is the quintessential opposite of the methods everyone else uses, you will be successful."

John thought that the Marketing Master was exaggerating just a tad here. "Wait a minute," he said. "Are you telling me that the successful companies do their service coaching totally differently from all the service 'amateurs' and that this difference stayed unnoticed for years or even decades of management training?"

"Yes, that is exactly what I'm telling you," replied the Master. "And it's easy to prove. When I start coaching a new client, I always meet the CEO first, and he or she gives me an introduction on how they do business. I always ask about the company's mission statement and their service philosophy and—equally important—who developed it. Very often, I get answers like, 'Our service philosophy was developed by the service department and external consultants' or I hear something like 'We did market research first and then asked our clients what they wanted. On that basis, our board of directors, the service department, external consultants, and a group representing our employees jointly developed our service philosophy.' But whenever I hear a description like that, I turn to the CEO and respond with something akin to the following: 'I'll bet that you developed a wonderful brochure with a classy design about your service standards. You introduced it to your employees at an impressive event. They've all received a brochure, read it, and placed it at a prominent place on their desk. But you're not happy with the way they responded to it, am I right?'

"I always get a strong 'yes' at that point. Indeed, a few months ago, one CEO asked me, 'How do you know our company that well?' I answered, 'I don't know your company that well at all. But I know that the service process you just described to me has proven to be completely ineffective time after time. Therefore, I know that the results for your company couldn't have been much better.'

"This CEO looked at me with an expression of surprise and said, 'Okay, let's pretend that our approach was all wrong. How would you have done it, and why am I supposed to believe that we would have achieved a great service culture using your methods?'

"I said to him, 'You did the best you could, given the advice you were given. But there is no reason to pretend that your procedure did in fact work. Your results have already proven to you that this approach didn't achieve what you were looking for. And the results of this method in any other company that installs service standards from top to bottom are inevitably equally disappointing.' Then I told him how I had learned years ago how to turn that change-management process completely around.

"Over a decade ago, I attended an international workshop for marketing consultants in California. Some of the world's leading experts met there for a week and exchanged their best case studies and coaching examples of how to support their clients in marketing.

"I had my first presentation on the first day at 2:00 in the afternoon. The gentleman who had given his presentation before me had taken away all the flip chart markers. I realized this only about five minutes before my speech started. I left the room and saw a waiter who was carrying a huge platter to deliver room service. Since I was under such extreme time pressure, I asked him for some markers, but I really didn't expect any help because I knew he had to finish his job of delivering lunch. Instead of rejecting me or explaining that he had to do something else, he answered very politely, 'I can deliver your markers in about three minutes. Will that solve your problem?' I nodded; he smiled warmly and proclaimed 'You're welcome.' And he delivered the markers on time, as promised and thus solved my problem.

"Three days later, I was standing in the sixth floor with a friend from Switzerland in the gallery, overlooking the hotel's reception area. We saw a guest arrive in a wheelchair. He had problems passing through the revolving doors. The porter and all the receptionists were busy, so nobody was there to help this gentleman. All of a sudden, we saw the guy cleaning the windows climb down from the top of a thirty-foot ladder, wipe his hands dry, approach the guest in the wheelchair, and personally direct him to a more convenient access door.

"My friend from Switzerland asked me, 'How many hotels do you know where someone from the gardening or cleaning staff would have the awareness to see that this guest needed help? And of those who noticed, how many would have interrupted their work and helped the guest, since it wasn't their job in the first place?' I concurred with my friend and explained that the employees of this hotel obviously didn't define their jobs in terms of their specific function of being a waiter, a gardener, or a cleaner. While those may be the functions they are primarily assigned to do, they all know that their ultimate 'task' is making their guests happy. I suggested finding the hotel manager and interviewing him about his secrets.

"Later that week, the opportunity presented itself to talk to the director of the hotel. I complimented him on the excellent service and I asked him how he trained his staff to implement this wonderful five-star service. He started giving me a long speech about how the service program wasn't really that special and that he was facing a lot of challenges because he couldn't pay his people as much as he wanted to. He said the variations in service quality were very high, that many of the service people came from other countries, and how some of them even had difficulties understanding and speaking English.

"The longer the list of his handicaps became, the more I was impressed that he achieved that wonderful service standard anyway. So I asked again how he did it specifically. I'll never forget his answer. *'It wasn't anything special. The only thing that we are truly proud of is that we implanted our service culture into our people in a period of less than two years. Because of the low salaries, we can't demand much from our employees in the service departments, so we tried to keep the process as simple as possible. We got all employees together and put them into teams with the same function. All of the gardeners in one group, the kitchen staff in one group, the housekeepers in one group and so on. And then we asked each team one specific question:* ***Imagine that you were a guest in our hotel. How would you know from the specific behavior of our housekeepers that you were not only a customer, but that you were our honored VIP guest for whom we would constantly go the extra mile?'"***

The Master stopped abruptly, looked at John, and said, "Do you have any idea why the structure of this question is so incredibly powerful?"

John thought for a moment and said, "I think the power comes from the change of perception. The housekeepers began to look at their job not just from their own perspective, but from the critically relevant perspective of the customer."

"That is right!" exclaimed the Master. "That is the first powerful element in this structure. But there is another important point here, namely that is even more helpful to actually put things into practice and really assist employees to change and improve their behavior. And that very strong effect is triggered by the phrase ***'How would you know from the specific behavior of our housekeepers?'*** This means the housekeepers were not just discussing in the abstract the typical service concepts of friendliness, politeness, and willingness to help. They were required to ***describe, from a guest's perspective, the specific behavior*** of housekeepers in specific contexts. For example, one housekeeper stated the following: 'When I'm in a rush to go to an appointment, I would like the housekeepers to greet me with a nice, energizing smile, say hello, and tell me to have a wonderful day. And when I'm more relaxed, I would like them to take personal interest in me and my situation, perhaps ask whether I am here on a vacation and whether I might have a chance to visit Sea World or something like that."

The Marketing Master paused and said to John, "After having coached the German national coaches for our Olympic and world champion teams for eight years, I know one thing to be certain: If an athlete does not have a crystal-clear, detailed picture of the movements he is going to make, chances are he will not fully internalize the process and most likely not perform at his optimal level. ***Crystal-clear, detailed visualizations are the prerequisite for our mind to perform complex behavior.*** If you can't picture yourself performing, say, a forward flip, you simply won't be able to do it.

"The importance of this visualization of specific behavior became very clear to me when the hotel manager invited me to look at the brainstorming ideas of the different groups of employees. For example, one gardener said, 'If I arrived at this hotel with my eight suitcases and the outside temperature was a hundred degrees and I saw the gardener riding his lawn mower around the roses instead of helping me, I would be angry. But if he sees me, interrupts his work, and helps with my luggage, he would be going an extra mile for me.'

"Each group of employees came up with similar situation descriptions, precisely pinpointing what five-star service behavior would look like to them. ***So they learned to define their jobs not from the function of cleaning rooms or driving tractors, but from the contexts of how they could interact with guests to make them happy and feel at home.***

"They learned that different employees may have different functions, but that the job of every employee in every five-star company is to make its guests happy. It is as complex and as simple as that."

John was very impressed and wrote down the following:

- To implement a service culture, make your employees work together in teams with other employees who share the same function.

- Ask each team only one question: *If you were a customer/client of our company, how would you know from the specific behavior of our receptionists, bookkeepers, sales staff, etc. that you were not only a customer, but a highly welcome VIP guest for whom our service professionals would walk the extra mile?*
- Make sure that people describe specific behavior in specific contexts that can be visualized. New crystal-clear inner "movies" are the prerequisite for new behavior!

John handed his note to the Master and said, "It can't be that easy. There must be more to it."

The Master looked at John's summary and said, "No, you listed the action steps perfectly. If you want, I'll add a few reminders for you about the overall picture."

- Changes in processes don't work from the top down. They only work from the bottom to the top.
- To be successful, you have to include all employees in the process; even people not present when their colleagues did the brainstorming were later provided an opportunity to add their input.
- The most important rule behind this is: **Identification requires participation.**
- This means if you have 8,000 employees, everyone has to participate and offer his or her ideas on how to improve the service standards. If you are too impatient to take a few months to get this process done, don't do it at all: People who don't identify with what they are asked to do won't internalize the new standards.
- Rewards and punishments are weak motivators compared to **identification.**
- Don't focus on the change process itself in your communication. Change is a means to an end. Focus on the vision, the visualization of the outcome when it's already achieved.

"There is one question that keeps coming to my mind," John said as he read his notes. "When you ask your employees about the ideal standard of behavior, do you fear that they are bright enough only to describe standards other than the ones you were hoping for because they are setting their own standards against which their own performance will be judged? Isn't it just human behavior to not set your own standards too high and end up with even more work than before?"

"I understand this fear. It is the reason why most entrepreneurs never start to really include their people in change-management processes. The interesting thing, though, is that everybody who is willing to try this method has found the opposite to be true. Most people want to be proud of themselves and therefore want to do outstanding jobs. The fifteen-year-old elevator boy in our example loves to be complimented by his guests for his great service. The tips he receives are only part of his compensation. When someone feels that he is appreciated for the outstanding service he delivers, he is far more motivated to be a great employee in a five-star hotel than in a two-star hotel where guests may not even recognize that he is there. The truth about this process is that employees become so enthusiastic that they usually suggest much more excellent service ideas than you would have implemented in the first place. A strong manager will collect all their suggestions and then make sure that the team has the chance to realize them one step at a time.

"What do you think about a fifteen-minute break?" the Master suggested with a grin, observing John's less-than-energized body posture. "Then I have another wonderful management process for you that varies by 180 degrees from what most managers practice in their businesses. Would you be interested in turning your employees into a high-performance team that can solve problems in thirty minutes, in contrast to other companies that need days and still are not successful?"

John grinned; the Master and his promises never failed to capture his attention. Energized, he walked outside and inhaled the wonderful fresh mountain air. *Hmmm, perhaps this fresh air is one of the secrets to all of these ideas,* he mused as he drifted off into a restless, mid-afternoon nap.

2. How To Triple Your Team's Effectiveness in Problem-solving by at Least 300 Percent

"You seem to have a lot of fun finding marketing processes that are totally different from what everyone else is doing." John started the conversation after the break, expressing his curiosity about the Master's last promise.

"It's true that a lot of what really works is very different from conventional marketing wisdom, but I'm not looking for techniques and tools for the sake of being different. To me, the main rule of marketing is testing, testing, and then testing again. The market and the client are always right. One's theories may sound great and they may even be worth a Nobel Prize. But if they don't help drawing clients to you, they are not worth the paper they are written on. What I'm really looking for is what withstands the test of the market, and paradoxically, this is often completely different from conventional wisdom.

"Let me give you another example. Over my lifetime, I have worked closely with hundreds of companies. I have seen four different entrepreneurial styles. I met entrepreneurs who were:

- thinking small and acting small
- thinking small and acting big
- thinking big and acting small, and
- thinking big and acting big.

"Which of those four groups do you believe had the most successful entrepreneurs?"

John said, "That is not very difficult. Thinking and acting small gets you nowhere, thinking small and acting big is still restricted by your thinking. Thinking big but acting small is the right direction, but restricted by small acting. So the winner is thinking big and acting big!"

"You are right about the thinking big. But when you work long enough with dozens and dozens of companies, you find out that those who try to act big usually take a bigger piece of the pie than they can chew and digest. The winner is thinking big and acting small. Thinking big and relentlessly taking all the small steps each and every day is the key to success. This has been proven right by my American colleague, Jason Jennings. He worked for years on documenting that the one-tenth of 1 percent of American companies that practice this philosophy are the ones that grow the most over years and decades. So the question is in knowing this, how can you put this into practice? And the answer is that you use your brain and your employees' brains in a way that differs by 180 degrees from what your teachers told you. Let's zoom in for a moment on the wrong approach that you find everywhere when marketing and sales are not performing well:

- Step 1: Whenever sales are going down, you can bet that the head of the sales department will ask his people **for more action**—working longer and harder.

- Step 2: If more action doesn't work, the next step is to ask **for better organization** of the resources—the reason why a lot of companies are constantly reorganizing.

- Step 3: If reorganizing doesn't work either, the board usually calls **for new solutions**—we need to *think outside the box* is the credo in this phase. That is usually the phase where things get difficult and external experts are often hired. Being one of those experts, I get a lot of typical briefings in step 3. They usually focus on …

- Step 4: The budget and other restrictions are the reasons why they did not achieve what they had set out to. With that information and still not knowing what they had set out to do in the first place, I was in no position to help them yet. To get out of this mess, I would usually ask them the following question.

- Step 5: 'What do you want to achieve in the long run?' I asked them to describe to me in detailed pictures what things would look like after reaching their objectives. Sometimes what they described to me made sense. At other times, they said things like 'We want to double the percentage of clients who recognize our brand.' Every time I didn't understand their objectives, I asked them the next step:

- Step 6: 'Why do you want to achieve this?' In other words, what is your intention behind this goal?

"Would you agree so far that most marketing and management processes to find new solutions to old problems would take this order?" The Master looked to John for confirmation.

"Oh, absolutely," John answered quickly. "In all of the companies I've worked for before I became self-employed, the mantra with problems was always 'take more action.' If that didn't work, the next step was usually better organization, and then, new solutions. I think we usually got stuck in the phase of new solutions, because we rarely came up with breakthrough new concepts that worked much better than the old ones."

"Very good observation, John," commended the Master. "You are exactly right. It took me years of observation, a few workshops on creativity, and the support of the American productivity expert David Allen, who wrote a brilliant book on how to get things done, to find out that we have been trained since childhood to think exactly the opposite of the way that our mind works naturally. Therefore it is no wonder that even the most intelligent people are performing poorly when it comes to solving marketing or sales problems (or, for that matter, any kind of problem). Think of a three-year-old who watches his dad washing the car on Saturday morning. All of the sudden, the little guy's mind comes up with an intention:

- Step 1—Intention: 'I would love some ice cream now.' (Maybe he saw a friend on the other side of the street eating ice cream.)
- Step 2—Pictures of the desired end result: 'Mmmm, licking this strawberry-flavored cone would taste so good.'
- Step 3—Intuitive survey for limitations: 'If I ask my dad, he will be angry. He doesn't like interruptions when he washes the car.'
- Step 4—Brainstorming for solutions: 'Who could I ask? Mom isn't here. But Grandmother? Cool idea!'

- Step 5—Organizing ideas into a practical action format: 'If I ask Grandmother and Dad hears it, he will be against it. So I'll ask her in the kitchen.'
- Step 6—Action steps: Walking over to the kitchen, looking for Grandmother, asking her with his nicest voice: 'Grandma, would you do me a favor? It is so hot outside ...'

"Do you get the picture?" The Marketing Master looked at John to ensure he was following.

"Wow, that is exactly the process my brain uses all day to find solutions," John blurted out excitedly, a little astonished about discovering this thought process. "I just remembered how I planned for our wedding. This was precisely the process I followed:

- Step 1—I was engaged to my wife and we wanted to get married a few weeks later, but I had this burdensome feeling because I didn't know my parents-in-law very well.
- Step 2—I had pictures in my head of a dinner with only the four of us. I saw us in a nice restaurant and my father-in-law sharing experiences from the time he and my mother-in-law got engaged. We were drinking red wine, and when we proposed a toast, he suggested the old tradition from Switzerland of clinking our glasses.
- Step 3—My mind started racing. 'You are a student. You don't have very much money. If the dinner costs more than $200.00, you will be well beyond your budget for the month.'
- Step 4—My mind started immediately going through all the restaurants I knew in the area that might be nice enough and still affordable. I finally came up with a nice Italian restaurant and a sushi bar.
- Step 5—I organized the solution: Checking which one was open on Monday when my father-in-law had the day off.
- Step 6—Making the reservation for the Italian restaurant and inviting my parents–in-law by phone."

"This is a great example," the Marketing Master complimented John. "That is exactly the way our mind works and activates its creativity to organize tons of ideas. But if you do it the other way round, you get stuck in the phase of generating new ideas!"

"Why is that?" John wanted to know.

"As long as your mind doesn't know the intention of what you are looking for and has no pictures of the desired results and no framework of the project's limitations, you cannot access your creativity. Here's an example. Once I was approached to do some marketing consulting. During the first meeting, the CEO presented to me a simple four-page flyer, as well as a very stylish, high-quality, twenty-page flyer and asked me in a demanding tone of voice, 'Now tell me, in your opinion, which one is better for our company?'

"I had no idea what to say. Finally I replied, 'That depends on what you want to use it for. Is it something you give away at conventions or is it something you want to use with highly qualified, pre-selected prospects?' He answered, 'I truly have no idea what our marketing department wants to use it for.' I said, 'As soon as you know, you will know intuitively which brochure will be better for the intended purpose.' So please keep this in mind, John: ***To activate our creativity to produce practical solutions, we need to provide our mind with a specific context.***

"This insight, by the way, heightened my awareness and allowed for me to make a very powerful conclusion: The rule of thumb is ***the more a company speaks in general terms about service or quality, the worse the quality or the service generally is.*** But the more they use context specific examples of service, such as 'we offer each guest of our hotel a glass of champagne when they check in,' the greater the chances that this idea will be realized."

John was very impressed, but couldn't resist asking one more question. "When our natural creativity flows effortlessly from phases one to six, as you described, how can it be that problem-solving processes in business are done exactly the other way around?"

"Honestly, I don't know," the Marketing Master replied with a huge grin, "but my assumption is that our teachers did it to us. Remember your

English teacher? Didn't he teach you to write the outline first and then the story? And then you sat in front of a white piece of paper, having no idea what the structure could be. Finally, with the time ticking away, you left the first page empty and simply wrote your story. In the end, you looked at the outline you had chosen intuitively and filled it in on the first page."

John grinned and said, "How do you know me that well?"

"That's easy," the Master responded. "It seems that teachers all over the world play this silly game. And after you grew up and became an entrepreneur, your banker wanted to see your business plan. Yet every business plan I've ever seen was basically useless. The ones that worked were developed in many feedback loops testing the reactions of the market. Then they were put together in hindsight and offered to bankers naïve enough to believe that it was the original plan."

John intuitively felt the wisdom behind the observations of the Marketing Master. *Maybe he exaggerates a bit,* he thought, *but he really has his finger on the pulse of the industry in general.* He wrote in his manual:

How to lead your team through problem-solving processes with 300 percent effectiveness: Reverse the order of normal business discussions to the natural creativity process of the mind.

- Step 1: Intention—Start with the end in mind: What do you intend to achieve?
- Step 2: Pictures of desired end result: Think big—How do things look and feel when everything is achieved?
- Step 3: Conscious and subconscious limits: What are the limits, hurdles, handicaps, and challenges we have to master?
- Step 4: Brainstorming of solutions within the framework of a context: How could it be done?
- Step 5: Prioritize and organize: How can these ideas be organized into a powerful plan of action?
- Step 6: Action: What is the first step?

The Master looked at John's list and said, "Well done, John. You deserve a wonderful weekend in the mountains. I'll meet you Monday morning at 10:00 AM for the last three magnets. We'll start with the power of persuasion.

John was a little exhausted when he arrived at his hotel. He took a two-hour nap and woke up very refreshed—but with only one hour left before his appointment at BMW! John was going to test drive the new M5. He was trying it out on the German Autobahn with no speed limit. *Maybe I'd better write in my diary now or I won't do it at all today,* he thought. Next he wrote:

- Do a workshop with the whole team.
- Divide them into small groups according to their function.
- Ask every group only one question: *If you were a client of our company, how would you know by the specific behavior of e.g. the salesperson that he or she really appreciates you as a client and gives you VIP service?*
- Allow every group to brainstorm on this question and fine-tune their answers until they are sure they developed a five-star service concept they are proud of.
- Allow each team to write down their ideas and put them into a service contract. Invite each team member to sign the contract as a founding member.
- Tell them that new team members will be only hired if they accept the code of conduct agreed upon by the founding members.
- Celebrate with the whole team!

Chapter 6: The Fifth Heart Magnet: Magnetic Selling: Tripling the Power of Persuasion

John rose especially early this morning. His plan was to go for just a quick jog, but he decided to take the opportunity to enjoy the sheer beauty of this crisp spring morning and take in the magnificent views of the snow-capped mountains. He ran for an hour and felt totally energized and ready to take on the challenges of the day. It was precisely 9:59 AM when he rang the doorbell to the Marketing Master's office. He was greeted with a huge smile. The Master said, "How was your weekend? Are you ready for some action?"

"Oh yes! My weekend was beyond wonderful. I went to Garmisch-Patenkirchen, then to Innsbruck, and finally Bozen. It's amazing to be able to shop in three different countries on the same day, only an hour's drive to Austria and another hour to Italy. That's so cool!"

"I'm curious to find out your opinion about the different salespeople you met," the Master said as he seized on the perfect opportunity to lead into the coaching topic of the day.

"I don't recall anything special. It was pretty much what I would consider normal and reasonably nice. Actually, there was this one guy in a sports store in Innsbruck who was really great at selling me a tennis racket, which was sort of interesting because I already have more than a dozen of them."

"Well now, that is interesting. Why did you decide that you needed another racket when you already own so many?" the Master asked.

"Well, if you know people who are truly passionate about tennis, then you know that they are never happy with the rackets they own. They always believe that the racket they buy next could lead them to the big breakthrough they have been dreaming of for years. But this time, it was different. I really didn't want to buy anything. I was only looking. Then this young salesman approached me and asked me a few questions, starting with, 'Have you ever had any problems with tennis elbow?' When I responded that I had, he asked me if I had ever told my doctor the cause of it. I explained to him that I had told my doctor that every time that I hit the ball, I felt a micro-shock to my elbow. When I play too much, it seems to add up over time and then the pain kicks in.

"He replied, 'Well, imagine if the micro-shock could be reduced. How much reduction would you wish for to be on the safe side to avoid tennis elbow in the future?'

"'I don't know exactly,' I told him. 'But I do know that when I reduce my training time by about a third during the off season, my arm is always fine.'

"The salesman continued, 'What if I told you that there is a racket utilizing cutting-edge titanium technology that was originally developed for ski racers and that that technology would reduce the impact of hitting the ball by 62 percent? Do you think your elbow would like that?'

"'That would be a dream come true,' I said, completely excited.

"The young man added, 'Just think about your next tennis lesson. What would using such a racket do for you, even before you stepped onto the court to hit your first ball?'

"'My fear of injury would be reduced in an instant and I would really go for it and play hard instead of always holding back the last 10 percent,' I said.

"The young guy nodded in agreement, reached over, and handed me their newest racket from Völkl. 'This racket has 62 percent less shock impact than any of the other top rackets,' he said. 'They used the technology of their racing skis. Perhaps now you can understand why a small country like Austria consistently produces some of the greatest skiers in the world.'

"And after he said that, I was sold. I absolutely needed that racket," John said, still impressed with the sales experience.

"That's a great story, John, and it's actually an example of how you sold yourself," the Marketing Master explained, "and that is exactly what we are talking about today when it comes to magnetic selling.

"But let me ask one question up front: When you think about this young salesperson who convinced you that this new racket would be good for you by preventing injuries and increasing your confidence, would you agree that he stuck out from the other salespeople you met during your shopping tour?"

"Oh, for sure," John agreed wholeheartedly. "This guy really added value. I didn't even know that this technology existed and that it could improve my career as a tennis player."

"Well, that is the first point I want to make today," the Master explained. "*Excellent persuasion is a client attractor in and of itself.* It is obvious that a sales team with good persuasion skills helps company sales, but more importantly, **it is a client attractor when it is done right. It touches our hearts and invites us strongly to buy—therefore I call it Magnetic Selling."**

"What would be an example of using persuasion skills in the wrong manner?" John asked, not exactly sure where the Master was heading.

"Well a lot of salespeople still use old 'pushing' techniques from the days of hard selling. Indeed, there are still many sales trainers out there coaching them to do so. We already talked about it last Monday. The problem with that is, people are sick and tired of getting products shoved down their throats. And when you start inviting clients with the other magnets, hard selling backfires even more.

"Imagine you are going to see a dentist who is the leading expert in implantation technology. He was recommended to you by word of mouth by a good friend. You visit his office and enjoy the inviting environment and his friendly team. But if the doctor shows up and starts giving you a sales pitch like a snake oil salesman, wouldn't that be annoying?"

"It would be more than annoying. I honestly would start doubting his expert status and tell myself that maybe he wasn't as good and as sought-after as I thought. If he were as highly in demand as I thought, he wouldn't need to be that pushy."

"That's what I'm pointing out here," the Marketing Master agreed. "The more you use magnetic marketing techniques, the more counterproductive it is when your sales team still uses old pushing techniques."

"So the challenge becomes how do I teach them Magnetic Selling and coach them to be as good as that guy in that Innsbruck sporting goods store, who could have sold me anything?" John wanted to know.

"It's easier than you might think. First, you explain to them the most important paradigm on persuasion—the power of self-persuasion, as I will explain more in a minute. Second, you teach them how to ask a set of five different types of clarifying questions. Shall we experience it in action?"

"Yeah, I know your strategy of making things look easy. But I bet it isn't as easy as that!" John proclaimed, as he couldn't resist voicing some of his doubts.

"Oh, it is even easier than I told you." The Marketing Master's grin widened. "Because with Magnetic Selling, your sales team doesn't have to 'unlearn' anything that they already know and do. You just ask them to add another three to five questions to their sales presentation, and they will triple their effectiveness. Let's start with the paradigm shift."

1. The Most Important Paradigm on Persuasion

"What would be a practical example of this?" John wondered, not exactly sure whether he understood what the Marketing Master was talking about.

"Let's say you have a Caucasian friend who is deeply in love with an African-American woman. He shares with you that he has never told his parents about his relationship. So you ask him why he hasn't done so, and he says, 'I really can't tell my mom.' Now you could try to convince him that he could because even conservative parents have changed their mindsets over such an issue in the last couple of decades. You could even share a similar experience from your own life, where it was helpful that you finally shared what was going on. But chances are that your friend will think, 'Yeah, that might be true for *him.* But my mom is different. I just can't do that to her.'

"If instead you were to approach this situation from the perspective of influencing his self-talk, you might ask a different question, such as, 'What would happen if you did?'

See, somebody who is telling himself forever that he can't do something usually has no internal 'movies' in his mind. He has no tools showing him how doing something like this would feel to him. It doesn't make sense to him to develop these movies in the first place.

"Now, by asking that question, you force your friend to stretch his inner map. Maybe he says, 'She would have a heart attack.' And you say, 'Yes, that's one possibility. What else could happen?' And he may say that his parents would get mad at him and not show up at his wedding. Then you agree again and ask him what he thinks about how long they might not talk with him and he may say, 'Forever!' You could respond with, 'Yes, that's the longest time span that they could possibly go without talking to you. What other time frames could you think of where there is no communication? Which time frame do you think has the highest probability? If he then estimates, 'Chances are that my parents won't talk with me for a year', you could ask him, whether he loves his girlfriend enough to pay that price to be with her. Do you get the idea?" the Master asked John, to see whether his example made sense.

"You're saying that most people in persuasion processes *tell the other person what is most convincing on their own maps*. And it would be much more effective if they asked themselves, ***What can I say to invite my partner to change his cognitive map himself?'***

"That's exactly right. You got it. And that is the whole basis of the Magnetic Selling process. Let me just walk you through the different steps."

2. The five steps of Magnetic Selling: How to reach your buyer's heart by tripling your power of persuasion

"In Magnetic Selling, you use five different types of questions," the Marketing Master explained. He took a piece of paper and wrote on it:

- Step 1: Situation analysis
- Step 2: Strength analysis
- Step 3: Challenge analysis
- Step 4: Consequence discovery
- Step 5: Benefit discovery

"Should we go through an example first, so that you can experience for yourself how persuasion can be tripled in effectiveness?" The Master's offer was met with John's enthusiastic nod.

"Let's imagine that I was interested in offering you our Master Sales Training program. I would start with **step 1,** asking you some questions to explore the situation of your sales team. Possibly:

- 'John, how many people are on your sales team?'—'My team consists of roughly 100 people.'
- 'And how many sales presentations do they do every day?'—'Well they should do four presentations, but on average they do two.'
- 'How long have you been coaching your sales team, John?'—'I have built it over the last five years.'

"Moving to **step 2** gives you the opportunity to present some strengths of your team and invites you to show me where you are performing well. I would question you as follows:

- 'Wow, building that team over five years, you must know everything about them. John, tell me: What are the greatest strengths of your team?'—'Well, when I bought the company five years ago, they were not even average. But now they are very good at finding leads and they do excellent sales presentations.'

- 'That's very good. What is it that you are most proud of in your coaching?'—'We doubled sales over the last three years in an industry that lost, on average, about 25 percent of its customers in the same period of time.'—'Wow, that is really impressive. Let me guess. Knowing your industry pretty well, I assume that you were something like number one or number two on the list of the fastest-growing companies?'—'Yes, we were number two.'

"See, what I'm after here? When I ask you about your strengths, I first have the chance to compliment you sincerely, based on the positive facts you told me. Secondly, it is a good way to boost your self-confidence and get your ego out of the way before we get to the more delicate points. **Step 3** is to discover your challenges and determine whether we can offer something really valuable to you. I would use questions like: "John, I see your team is already playing in the Championship League of Sales. I'm guessing your goal is to take them to the Olympics. As good as your people are, is there anything you think they could improve upon?"

"Oh definitely," John replied. "They are superb when it comes to presenting. But when they receive objections that they should be able to handle, they are not even close to being masters. Sometimes I feel their closing techniques are completely inadequate."

The Master backed away from the demonstration and said, "Now I have a foundation of what your problems are. What do you think most sales coaches would recommend as the next step?"

John replied, "In all the seminars I've attended, I have learned that after you discover the problem, you present the solution."

"That's exactly what most old-fashioned sales models recommend, and as you know, it can and will get you into trouble fast. Let's just play with this and do it the wrong way.

"John, I can see that you need some serious sales training here. Our company provides world-class state-of-the-art sales training. When it comes to handling objections and closing sales, I can show you references of how we've helped our clients bring in 50 percent more sales."

"That sounds great. What would such a training program cost?"

"Well, it provides a very high value to your company, as you can see. So your investment would be $100,000 for the first module."

"Wow that is quite an investment. I should talk with my board of directors about it first."

The Master backed away from the demonstration again and said, "In this presentation, I told you how good our product is. I promised you 50 percent more sales, and you may have believed it or not. But your reaction told me that you are somewhat skeptical about whether our program is worth $100,000. Now let's do it using Magnetic Selling on my part. Let me show you **step 4**—the discovery of consequences.

"John, you've told me that your 100 salespeople do two presentations a day each. How many of those 200 presentations does your team close?"

"The average closing rate is 10 percent, so every day they bring in around twenty contracts."

"Now John, imagine that your salespeople were as good as you could imagine when it comes to handling objections and closing the sale. Of the 180 presentations left open, how many of them could be closed with the right techniques?"

John thought for a moment and said, "Good salespeople have a closing rate of roughly 15 percent, and those aren't even our best ones. So our team could easily close thirty presentations a day with the right techniques."

"Help me out here, John. Ten more contracts per day … how much would that add up to over the period of a year?"

"We have 240 selling days. So we would add a whopping 2,400 sales every year."

"As I know from before, you are selling investment funds. What is the average amount your clients sign up for?"

"It's around $30,000."

"Wow, that is a lot. I know that your industry calculates that with a minimum profit rate of 5 percent agio. Is that a fair guess?"

"Yes, it is."

"I'm not great with big numbers. Help me out here—2,400 sales times $1,500 profit, what does that amount to?"

John took out his calculator and was shocked by the numbers on the screen. "It would be an additional profit of $3,600,000 every year."

The Master stood again and asked John, "Do you remember last Monday when I told you: **People can refuse everything somebody else tells them. But they are completely open to that what they tell themselves?**

"With Magnetic Selling, I've invited you to discover the consequences of a good sales training program for yourself. You told yourself that you could close 15 percent of your customers instead of 10 percent. You told yourself that it would add up to an additional profit of $3.6 million per year. Would you agree that this approach could help in creating some excitement about the solutions I have to offer? And that you would take a very different value perspective on my services if you figured out on your own that it could make you more than $3 million per year?"

John was stunned. He was so excited that he could hardly speak. When he found his voice, he said, "That is the most powerful thing I have ever heard. When you invite your client to discover the consequences of their decision themselves, there will rarely be any objections; you really won my heart over. After calculating all that, I'm not interested in contradicting myself! So this is the time to present the solution."

"Not yet," the Master replied, "because, as my client, you are not only the best person to figure out why you lose an opportunity when you do not buy my sales training, but you are also the best when it comes to the next issue. Allow me to introduce you to **step 5**—discovering the benefits. The questions would be as follows.

"Now John, since you just figured out how costly it would be for your company to miss out on good sales training, tell me: If you found the ideal coaching concept for your team, what would be the biggest benefit to your company? I'm not only talking about $3.6 million in additional revenue at the end of the year. What would be the biggest benefit for each team member and your company as a whole, starting on the first day after the training?"

"Our biggest benefit would be the jump forward in self-confidence. We have a great new product that raises some questions on the part of our clients. If our people could handle them and increase their closing rate significantly, we would finally have injected the motivation I'm looking for."

The Master looked up again from the demonstration and said, "See, that's what I mean! Who am I to know what the greatest benefit of a sales training program is for your company? I wouldn't even have come up with the idea that it would be self-motivation, because so far you have only mentioned sales deficits. ***In Magnetic Selling, you guide your partner to figure out his losses if he doesn't buy from you and you help him to discover other benefits for doing so***. Only after that should your salespeople start their presentation! I'm not saying that they will close every client. What I'm saying is that after the client has explored for himself the consequences of not buying and the benefits of buying, you will have attracted him or her emotionally and will have turned the table as much in your favor as you could. How do you like that idea?"

"It is the best thing I ever heard of in the world of sales," John admitted, very impressed. "Could we go through that whole process again? I'd like you to give me some pointers to look for when I coach my team."

"Sure, that's why we are here!" The Master was thrilled at how quickly his student had grasped the concept.

Step 1: Situation analysis

Situation analysis involves asking the types of questions that even the average salesperson knows about, i.e., questions needed to analyze the current situation of your client. Example:

- What kind of tennis racket do you prefer?
- How many do you own?
- How often do you play tennis?
- What's your actual performance level?

Step 2: Strength analysis

"There is a very powerful type of question I developed years ago after a very frustrating experience whereby I missed out on the opportunity of closing a big sales deal. I was invited by the director of sales at a private bank in Hanover to give a presentation about our training concepts. After an introduction, I realized this gentleman had a rather large ego, shall we say. I started doing my analysis and wanted to figure out the strengths and weaknesses of his sales team. Whenever I asked him what improvements he would like to see in his team, he gave me a long speech to validate how great they already were doing.

"Because he had invited me to that meeting, I finally said, 'Okay, I understand your team is already fit to go to the sales Olympics. But since you invited me today to discuss a coaching program, I assume you want to make sure that they not only compete but that they actually win the gold medal. So please tell me, on the way to the gold medal or the world record, could your salespeople be even better?' At that point, after all my probing, he was really angry and said, 'You don't understand, my team is already great and we need no sales coaching at all.'

"I had a three-hour drive back to the airport, and enough time to figure out what went wrong and how I could do better the next time. The one thing I really did wrong was pretty obvious. Whenever I asked him about what his team could do better, he felt attacked and translated it into, 'Tell me what your team still hasn't mastered after you've coached them for years. Where did you fail?'

"At that moment, it dawned on me that we, as external experts, often pose a threat to the internal experts of the company. This is true of computer experts, consultants, and anyone else who offers a specific expertise to a company who may feel that they could or should have already provided the solutions to the company. Even the guy who explains better how to use a photocopy machine could be a threat to the head of technical equipment. His colleagues might think, 'If our guy were be as good as he pretends to be, he would have been able to make the copy machine work without external help.'

"Whenever you are going to ask your client what his problems are, he may not be revealing the whole truth, because he might fear that things will fall back on him and that he might be seen as part of the reason for the failure. That's the reason I invented the strength-analysis questions. With them, you invite your client to describe the strengths and successes he already enjoys. Questions like:

- What are you proud of as a tennis player?
- What are your best shots and strategies?
- An investment banker could ask his client which parts of his portfolio he was really happy with: What have been your best buying and selling decisions over the last few years?

"Those types of questions offer two huge advantages. Imagine the banker's client saying, 'I bought my Coca-Cola shares at exactly the same time Warren Buffett did.' That offers the opportunity for the investment banker to compliment his client in a very credible way. He can build the relationship and at the same time demonstrate his expertise.

"The more the client is invited to present where he is successful and strong, the more his ego gets out of the way. So when the banker tells him that a lot of professional investors would have been happy if they had had his great timing, the client is now seeing eye-to-eye with the banker. This adds enormously to his willingness to openly share the points he is less enthusiastic about in his portfolio."

Step 3: The challenge analysis

"The type of questions used in the challenge analysis is something your salespeople are already familiar with. They often call them problem-probing questions. At this stage, there is nothing much new to train your sales staff, except to remind them that they can't bore the client with the obvious questions only."

"What do you mean by that?" John wanted to know.

"It's well known that many novices don't ask enough questions. To compensate for that, many sales trainers drill their students with questioning techniques. The weaker salesperson learns that he is safe as long as he asks questions, because the client won't object to them. But the client may get bored, because everything the salesperson is asking in this phase, the client already knows. There is no room for discovery yet. Therefore the hallmark of seasoned, strong salespeople is that they ask very *elegantly only what they really need to know.* Typical questions in this area are:

- What is your problem?
- How many taxes did you have to pay last year?
- What is your biggest challenge in with regard to playing better tennis?
- What should the solution you are looking for be like in comparison to the product/service you are using now?"

Step 4: The discovery of consequences

"The big breakthrough for your salespeople to double or even triple their effectiveness comes when they master steps 4 and 5, as you saw in our example. Let me give you a couple of ideas on how to train your salespeople to find the right questions:

- First, ask them to make a list of the products and services your company has to offer.
- Second, let them list for each product all the problems your product or service can solve.

- Third, ask them to collect all the questions that would help your customer to identify the problems he has to deal with if he doesn't find a solution.
- Fourth and finally, it is usually very helpful for your client to figure out how much these problems cost him in monetary terms. The more he understands the consequences quantified in dollars, the easier it is for him to make a decision to invest in your product or service.

Step 5: The benefit discovery

"As you saw in my demonstration with you, it is pretty easy to invite your client to tell you what kind of benefits he would enjoy most. You simply ask him:

- Imagine that you've found a solution that really fits your needs. What would be your greatest emotional benefit? How would you feel from the first minute after owning that product/service?"

"This approach of Magnetic Selling is very powerful," John said, totally excited, "because you are basically watching as your client explores, with your guidance, what the consequences are in the event he doesn't buy from you. The second step is then to invite him to discover his highest benefits in using your product or service. The client is drawn to you like a magnet. That is the strongest persuasion strategy I've ever been introduced to!"

Magnetic Selling in handling objections

"Another important point about the structure behind Magnetic Selling is that you can very often use it to invite your client to handle his objections himself," the Master continued. "You usually do that by asking him a question that invites him to discover consequences he didn't see when raising his objection. Let me give you an example.

"Last year I was presenting the concept of Magnetic Selling to the sales director of one of the largest German insurance companies. He liked the presentation but wasn't very interested until I told him that this method would allow his salespeople to invite their customers to find the answers to the objections they raised themselves.

"So the sales director invited me to demonstrate this skill, which I did with enthusiasm. I told him to present one of the objections his sales staff hears every day yet seemed to have difficulty handling. He said, 'We have a private health insurance plan that completes the protection of the health policy provided by the public health care system. As part of the presentation, we explain that the customer would have access to the leading doctors and professors for his treatment. The most common objection is something like: 'That's impressive, but I really can't buy anything that extravagant only for the right to have a professor visit and shake hands with me every day.'

"My reply was, 'That's right, you can't buy anything for something as frivolous as a handshake. But you told me that you started your career as a lawyer. Imagine somebody suing you for millions of dollars in damages, potentially ruining your financial future. The law might be on your side, but it might be difficult to prove. Of the 100 students in your graduating class, how many would you trust to defend you in court if you weren't able to defend yourself? Your financial future depends on it."

John thought for a moment, grinned, and said, "Difficult question. You know how many get a degree these days without deserving it. I think I might trust three to five lawyers out of a hundred."

The Master continued, "Okay, then let's take out all the drama. This time your financial future is not on the line. Instead let's say you hurt yourself pretty badly playing tennis and you completely severed your anterior cruciate ligament. You know it would depend on the excellence of the surgeon as to whether your knee would get back to normal, as opposed to ending up with a 20 percent restricted movement. How important would it be that you had access to the three to five doctors who would be the choice of their own colleagues? Can you see now the importance of the advantage of the private health plan in providing access to the top experts in the field?"

John grinned and said, “Sold! I’ll get the program for my sales team!”

The Master turned to John. “Did you see the mechanism of discovering consequences in action here?”

“Oh yes,” John replied, “you asked him to access this mental map on how many experts there are out of a hundred people doing a job. Drawing from his own experience, he came up with the answer of three to five. After that, he couldn’t deny the advantage of having access to exactly this group of high-performing professors without contradicting what he said before.”

“You got it.” The Master smiled broadly. “Humans can always refuse what others tell them. But they are very open to being convinced by the things they tell themselves. Did you like the program today?”

“You really amazed me today. I honestly didn’t think that you could deliver on the promise that Magnetic Selling would triple persuasion effectiveness. But now I believe that inviting the client to deliver the answers from his own mental maps may even be five or even seven times more convincing.”

“Fabulous! Then don’t miss tomorrow. When it comes to self-motivation skills for you and your employees, I think we can do even better than a 300 percent increase.”

Later that afternoon, John was sitting again in his favorite Italian café. *Their latte is out of this world,* he thought ordering another one of their macchiatos. *They really accelerate my thinking,* he chuckled, opening his diary and writing down his insights from today:

- Train my sales and service people in Magnetic Selling.
- Teach them the paradigm shift that presenting world-class arguments is second best.
- It is best to invite the client by carefully drafting questions to make him argue himself why he needs and wants our product.
- Teach them the 3-S and 2-N questions.

- Most importantly: Teach them how to develop negative-consequence questions:
- List all our products and services.
- Ask for each product which of our customer's problems they can solve.
- Write down all these problems.
- Write down the questions that help uncover those problems.
- Make a list of possible consequences if those problems are not solved.
- Make a list of questions uncovering those consequences.

Chapter 7: The Sixth Heart Magnet: Motivation—Radiating eyes as a key attractor for clients (as well as team members and yourself)

John was off to an extra early start on this Tuesday morning. Looking out the window of his room, he saw the sun beginning to peek through the gorgeous mountains that were so prominent in his daily views throughout this trip. *Already Tuesday,* he thought, *another two days and I'll be back home. As strange as it felt at the beginning of my journey to follow my dreams and come here to get to the source of the Seven Magnets, it now seems that this beautiful lake town has quite comfortably become my second home over the course of the last week.*

Today was going to be another one of the power days. The Master had promised a breakthrough in self-motivation and how to teach it to his employees. "If it really works, not only for my team but also for myself, my wife will be really surprised upon my return. If I can find a way to get motivated to clean up the garage and the backyard!"

It was 9:50 AM when John rang the doorbell. When the Master opened the door with his customary huge smile, John thought to himself, *I've never seen this guy less than 100 percent motivated. If he really can teach others to reach that state of mind, I'm in for something very special today.*

"John, are you ready for a huge breakthrough?" the Master asked enthusiastically. "Would you like to find your individual recipe for self-motivation? It would enable you to motivate yourself literally for every goal and project you desire in just a matter of minutes, enough to motivate yourself for any task you haven't been able to undertake in decades."

John laughed out loud, musing about the Marketing Master and his bold promises. *There must be structure behind his mad claims,* he thought. *Maybe he just wants to confront me with my limited beliefs.* Even before he could answer, the Master continued, "John, let's think again about your shopping tour last Saturday. Can you remember how many stores you visited in total and how many of those stores made an impression on you?"

John thought for a moment and then replied, "I visited eleven shops, and two of them made a lasting impression on me."

"Describe what the difference was about those two."

"Well, the first one was the sports store that I already told you about. The other one was a bike store in Bozen, Italy. I didn't want to buy anything there either, but this shop had the coolest selection of mountain bikes I had ever seen in my life. In addition to the grand display, the saleswoman with whom I was talking made a distinct impression. She was definitely the most enthusiastic person I have ever met regarding mountain biking. I chatted with her for probably half an hour. She had ridden all of the different mountain bikes personally, and she explained to me the differences in terms of how each of them responded to conditions in difficult terrain."

"Were her eyes radiating and telling you that she loved what she was doing?" the Master asked with a big smile.

"No doubt about that. Her enthusiasm was so contagious that I ended up buying their brand-new front disc brake. I'm excited because I suspect I got it at least a year before they expect to begin exporting it out of Italy."

"Allow me one last no-brainer question before we start," the Master said with a huge grin. "Do you think her motivation will enable her to serve her clients better —and if so, do you think that this is an important component to touch the heart of her customers as well?"

"Absolutely, you can bet on it," John replied.

The Marketing Master continued. "Obviously, if an entrepreneur doesn't master the skill to motivate his team, a huge client attractor is missing. Not unlike persuasion and self-persuasion, all motivation is self-motivation. So the question becomes: ***What can you, the entrepreneur, do to invite your team members to be highly motivated every day and be totally enthusiastic about their jobs?***

"The answer is this: Because all motivation is self-motivation, giving pep talks to your employees won't change behavior very much. **But you can teach your employees how to find their personal hot buttons in order to motivate themselves.** And you can create an environment in your company whereby each employee can use some or all of their individualized personal motivators. I've taught this system for eight years to the German national coaches, and they've achieved extraordinary results in preparing their athletes for the Olympics and for world championships. So let's go for it!

"Let us start with correcting two big flaws most people have on their mental maps when it comes to self-motivation," the Master began:

- **Flaw number one** is that most people believe that they are not highly motivated; this is simply incorrect (and that works against them as a huge negative self-fulfilling prophecy): Everybody has some areas he or she is highly motivated in. Take yourself as an example. You told me that you are highly motivated when it comes to tennis and mountain biking, but that you have no discipline when it comes to cleaning the garage. The obvious truth is that ***people are highly motivated in some areas of their life, but they have difficulties in accessing that motivation in other areas.***

- **Flaw number two** is that people often define their *energy* potential from areas where they have difficulties motivating themselves; that inevitably leads them to the conclusion that they do not have enough energy to go after the things that they want. The truth is 180 degrees different. As you will soon find out, every human being has a few hot buttons for self-motivation; if any of these buttons gets pushed, we will be *motivated far beyond what is even good for us.*

"Think of road rage; there you have a very good example of how the 'competition' button, if pushed under the wrong circumstances, will 'motivate' very intelligent people to do very unintelligent things in order to 'win a fight' on the highway.

"So I suggest you forget this morning what you believe about your capability for self-motivation. Years ago, Charles Garfield, a famous American management coach, made me aware that Russian sports psychologists had found a secret weapon to teach their athletes about self-motivation for world-class performance. When I researched that concept more closely, I found that the Russians had a brilliant idea. They believed that when a world-class athlete had participated over a span of ten years in the Olympics, the world championships and the Russian championships and came up with, say, three personal records during this time, then *the events of the personal records may contain some very important information:*

- It could be that performing a new best in those events is purely accidental (or only due to a training peak)
- Or the reason for this new peak performance was that the athlete had *stronger motivation to achieve a* personal best.

"The Soviet scientists believed if the second alternative were true, then they should find recurring patterns that activated the personal best at each of the peak events. They interviewed and screened several hundred world-class athletes. To their surprise, their hypothesis held true: ***Whenever the athletes performed at their best, there were several hot buttons for self-motivation activated, which forced the athlete to perform beyond his previous limits.*** These buttons were different for different athletes. For example, some athletes told the researchers that their trainers didn't believe in them or that they were hurt before the event. That additional challenge gave them the extra drive to achieve a new record. Others reported that they had a new teammate they were competing against and that this activated their urge to win even more than usual. Then there were athletes who became inspired by other top performers they had watched, and they told themselves: 'If she can do it, I can do it as well.'

After evaluating their research protocol, and a few hundred interviews, the scientists discovered:

- There are fourteen different hot buttons for self-motivation that drive athletes to achieve peak performances.
- Each athlete usually has three to five buttons that work best for him.
- Each athlete had the same motivators activated through all the peak performances. The motivator buttons seemed to be very consistent and part of the athlete's personality.

"The Soviet psychologists then taught their athletes to activate their individual buttons for self-motivation consciously in their training environment on a daily basis. The results of that research made history. For over twenty years following this discovery in the 1970s, the world of sports was dominated in many disciplines by Russian athletes."

The Marketing Master paused to ensure John's mental participation and said, "Are you ready to find out your own individual recipe and hot buttons for self-motivation?"

"I can't wait to get started." John's voice vibrated with excitement.

"Great," said the Master, "then let me explain how you do it.

- First, make a list of three to five events where you performed at your best; please don't expect your successes to be as big as winning a gold medal at the Olympics. The key here is to find situations where you performed a lot better than you usually do. As we all know, we have days when we perform worse than our average. And then we have days when we have more energy, more motivation, and more endurance, and we achieve things we usually do not achieve; those are the events you are looking for.
- You can choose situations from business—for example, a project of yours that was a major success. You may choose examples of winning in your favorite sport. Or you can look at an example from home, such as building a great tree house for

your kids because you became inspired by the tree house your neighbor had built. Allow yourself five to ten minutes to select your examples.

- Next, arbitrarily decide which of the examples to analyze first. It really doesn't matter which one you take, so just take the one that attracts you most.
- Then sit back, relax, close your eyes, and remember the situation as vividly as possible. Look at it from three perspectives. First, see what you could have videotaped in that situation. Second, listen to your inner dialogue. What were you telling yourself to give such an outstanding performance? And third, look back from that situation. Was there anything in the phase of preparation that added to your motivation?
- After visualizing with closed eyes for about five to ten minutes, take a piece of paper and draw a mind map. Jot down everything that comes to mind about this situation, then circle the keywords and connect them graphically. That may take you another ten minutes. After that, we will take the notes of your first peak performance situation and analyze it together to determine your hot buttons for self-motivation.

"Do you have any questions about the process?" the Master wanted to know.

"Only one," John replied. "If I take a peak performance that took a longer time to achieve, let's say the six months in which I built our home with close to no help—where do I look there? Over the course of these six months, I was obviously very motivated at times, but at other times I was really down."

"Ahh, that's a great question. If your success was less of a one-time event and more of a process, you want to look at the final incident of this process when a lot of memories became condensed. So, for example, if you were analyzing the project of attaining your PhD, you may look at the day you defended your thesis."

John went to work. His mind was overflowing with ideas and finally he drew this mind map:

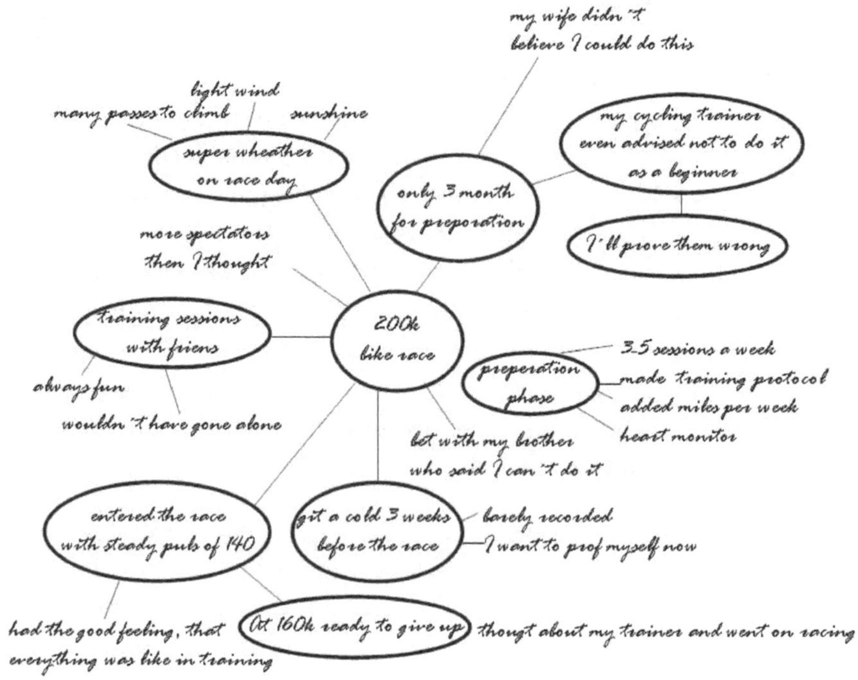

The master was impressed. "That's really a great job, John. You listed more than fifty keywords. That's an abundance of information that will make it easy for us to find your motivator buttons. Let's do it in three steps:

- First, I'll give you on overview of the fourteen motivator buttons the Soviet psychologists discovered.
- Second, you fill in the evaluation sheet.
- Third, I will show you how to use your individual motivation recipe to motivate yourself instantly for whatever project you choose.
- Fourth, we'll have a look at how you can use this knowledge to teach your team.

"Would that be a good investment of your time?"

John beamed with enthusiasm. "Let's go for it."

1. "The first motivator I want to introduce you to is **being in action.** What the Russians found here was that some of their athletes were thriving on the possibility of being in action. The more there was to do and the tighter the time schedule on the day of the competition, the higher the motivation and energy of the athletes. Another sign for thriving high on action is that these people found out about themselves, *the more they have to do on a given day, the more tasks they get done.* As paradoxical as it sounds, people motivated by action may already have five appointments on a given day, but if you give them eight additional calls to make, they get it done that day. Conversely, they may have not come around to do half of the calls on a more idle home office day."

2. "The second motivator button is being **inspired by examples.** Some athletes were more inspired and motivated by others who were already performing at the level these athletes were striving to achieve. The common thought there was: *if she can do it, I can do it as well.* Arnold Schwarzenegger was inspired by this motivator very much. As a young bodybuilder, his model of excellence was Reg Park. He tells in his autobiography that his next role model was Bill Pearl, and later on in his career, his models were the movie stars Sylvester Stallone and Clint Eastwood. Perhaps now it might be Ronald Reagan, who started as a governor of California before he became president of the United States," the Marketing Master added with a grin."

3. "The third motivator is **memories.** Remembering past successes or failures is, for many people, a very powerful motivator. Some athletes gained self-confidence and motivation by 'dwelling' on past successes; the more they thought about them and the more they visualized them, the more they built up the conviction: 'I can do this again.' Others reported that thinking about their failures gave them the 'kick' not to experience anything like it ever again. Marathon runners who had previously given up at

the twenty-mile 'wall' have reported that this experience from their early years was very inspiring to follow through whenever they had similar challenges later on in their careers."

4. **"Future perspective:** Some athletes reported that their motivation to perform at their personal best was strongly reinforced by the opportunity to invest in their future: 'If I compete successfully this time, I'm in the Olympics' or 'if I really train hard through winter preparation, I'll make it into the national team.' In general, people with this motivator are highly receptive to the promise of a better future: 'Working hard doesn't pay off today but there is a huge reward in the future waiting for me' is a strong driver for them."

5. **"Making sense** or **identifying with a task** is another powerful motivator. Some bookkeepers would never work for a tobacco company because they would be closely involved in producing cigarettes. The thought of supporting a company that shares the responsibility of others dying of lung cancer doesn't make any sense to them. What this motivator tells us then is how important it is for some people to have the short-term objectives of an assignment match their basic moral values. While some people need to know exactly why their work is useful (and they take pride in it working on important tasks), others are fine doing whatever they are told to, as long as they are paid appropriately. ('I do what I'm told to do. It's the responsibility of my boss to figure out whether it makes sense and what he needs it for.')"

6. **"Feeling good during the experience.** Some athletes performed at their best when they had to overcome the highest amounts of tension. While these athletes where thriving on extra amounts of stress and performed best under pressure, others were wired exactly the opposite way. They needed significantly less pressure than normal to achieve their personal peaks. The researchers concluded from this discovery that a certain amount of pressure (how much depends on the individual) is conducive to our peak performance. Managers understand this concept well. Many projects don't move well in the beginning because

the deadline is too distant and the pressure too low. When the schedule gets tighter, the motivation increases and things get done. So the key to using this motivator is to be aware of how much pressure we need to perform at our personal best and to generate this stress level in our lives wherever we want to perform well."

7. **"Competition.** There are two types of competition. First, there is the competition against others, the desire to be number one, the wish to win the game and beat the opponents. But there is also the game to compete against one's previous records. Some athletes are much more motivated to focus on a new personal record, a need to outperform themselves by the desire to outperform somebody else."

8. **"Working alone.** For some people, it enhances their motivation if they can do things alone. The opportunity to do things their way, at their own rhythm and with the freedom to create new things the way they like it, without being forced to compromise with suggestions from teammates, is a huge motivator to these individuals. This driver includes the wish for power over people. Being the leader of a group, having the power to tell people what to do, and feeling rewarded by the opportunity to do so are all further expressions of this motivator."

9. "An individual driven by **companionship** is motivated by the opportunity to get things done as a member of a group. The key factor here is not the capability of being a team player, nor is it the team spirit itself. It is how much somebody is motivated to follow through and achieve a peak result by the fact that he is working together with others to achieve the desired result. Think of exercise bikes, for example. Some people have no problem being disciplined and riding them in the gym, where there are others doing the same. But if they have one at home, it collects dust and is never used. The reason is not lack of character or missing discipline; the reason is that the powerful companionship motivator of these individuals is not activated when alone at home."

10. "**Factors from the environment.** For some marathon runners, a big crowd cheering them is a huge motivator for them not to give up during the last miles of the race. Whether it is the size of the group, the fact that the weather is good, because your parents are watching you, or because you are working at a new desk, some individuals are highly motivated by such environmental factors, whereas these factors are a lot less important to others."

11. **"Recognition.** We all want and need to be complimented and recognized and praised, but some of us are a lot more receptive and motivated by recognition than others. To some of us, being praised by our parents, our peers, or the public is one of the most powerful motivators of all. This driver also includes the wish for self-recognition. Some athletes, for example, told the researchers that it was more important to them to prove a certain performance to themselves. One person was quoted as saying, 'I would have hated myself if I hadn't achieved this.'"

12. **"Process feedback.** For some athletes, the feedback by other people, their appraisal and their compliments, was less important than the feedback from the training process itself. 'Seeing the progress I'm making during the training is more inspiring and more rewarding than all compliments in the world,' one gold-medal winner told the research team. 'I visualize even the smallest progress by creating graphs and pictures and that really keeps me on track.'"

13. **"Challenge.** 'You can't do it!,' 'You are too old (or too young)' or 'No one has ever accomplished it!' were some of the most powerful thoughts to challenge athletes. 'When my coach didn't believe in me, I had to prove that I could do it. That was always my greatest motivator,' one athlete was quoted saying. The Italian ski racer Alberto Tomba was known for his incredible second runs. 'Whenever he underperformed in the first run, chances were that he would demoralize his competitors in the second one,' his coach stated in a TV interview. So hardship of any kind—bad weather, injuries, lack of trust from the public or relevant peers—can and will work for some people as excellent motivators."

14. **"Preparation.** One last and very interesting factor the Russian psychologists learned from interviewing their best athletes was that they all need a different degree of preparation to achieve their personal best. Some athletes performed best when their preparation was meticulously detailed and nothing was left to surprise, while others performed better with a lesser degree of preparation allowing for more spontaneity and creativity during the process."

The Master looked at John and said: "So, now after you know what took the Russians years to develop, you are ready to find out your most powerful motivators in less than three minutes. Take this evaluation sheet and determine your motivators from the success example you just analyzed. Fill in your strongest motivators first, then look for your weakest ones, and fill in the middle ones last."

John looked at the sheets the master handed over to him. They looked like this:

Important — unmportant

		1	2	3	4	5
1.	Being in action:	○	○	○	○	○
2.	Inspired by examples:	○	○	○	○	○
3.	memories:	○	○	○	○	○
4.	Future perspective:	○	○	○	○	○
5.	Making sense or identifying with a task:	○	○	○	○	○
6.	Feeling googe druing the experience:	○	○	○	○	○
7.	Competition:	○	○	○	○	○
8.	Working alone:	○	○	○	○	○
9.	Companionship	○	○	○	○	○
10.	Factors from the enviroment:	○	○	○	○	○
11.	Recognitation:	○	○	○	○	○
12.	Process feedback	○	○	○	○	○
13.	Challenge	○	○	○	○	○
14.	Preperation:	○	○	○	○	○
15.	Other motivators:	○	○	○	○	○

John filled in the blanks and said, "These are my motivators, no doubt about it. But how can I use this to jump start my motivation for a new project?"

He handed the Master his profile.

		Important				unmportant
		1	2	3	4	5
1.	Being in action:	○	⊗	○	○	○
2.	Inspired by examples:	○	○	⊗	○	○
3.	memories:	○	⊗	○	○	○
4.	Future perspective:	○	○	○	○	⊗
5.	Making sense or identifying with a task:	○	○	⊗	○	○
6.	Feeling googe druing the experience:	○	○	○	⊗	○
7.	Competition:	○	⊗	○	○	○
8.	Working alone:	○	○	○	○	⊗
9.	Companionship	⊗	○	○	○	○
10.	Factors from the enviroment:	○	⊗	○	○	○
11.	Recognitation:	○	○	○	⊗	○
12.	Process feedback	⊗	○	○	○	○
13.	Challenge	⊗	○	○	○	○
14.	Preperation:	○	⊗	○	○	○
15.	Other motivators:	○	○	○	○	⊗

"That's great, John! Your main motivators are:

- challenge
- process feedback, and
- companionship.

Is there any project right now, personal or business, where you would like to increase your motivation tremendously to test your motivators?"

John thought for a moment before he answered. "Yes, in sports I would like to follow through and go for regular bike rides, as I have promised myself for years. In business I would like to increase the number of leads we get every month by at least 50 percent!" "Cool," the Master replied, "that's really easy to do. Let's start with your biking. What could we determine to be a nice challenge for you to achieve by the end of the season?"

"There is a twenty-four-hour, three-hundred-mile bike ride some of my friends take part in every September, which would be a tremendous stretch for me," John thought out loud.

"Do your friends believe that you could be ready for that challenge in four months?"

"No, usually you prepare for two years before you attempt it."

"Then doing it at the end of the first season would be a tremendous stretch, wouldn't it?" the Master asked.

"Oh, definitely," John said. "It would be an amazing accomplishment."

"Okay, so there's the challenge. Now let's look at companionship. Wouldn't it be much more fun to do your bike rides with some like-minded friends? Wouldn't it be easier for you to follow through with your program if you had committed to meet your friends on Monday, Wednesday and Friday at 6:00 PM for a two-to-four-hour ride?"

"For sure. Whenever I give my word, I keep it," John affirmed strongly.

"Well then, sounds like we have the challenge and that you have the companionship. Now all you need to do is include process feedback. Here's an idea: Why don't you get yourself a heart monitor and document each of your training units. Write down how many miles you bike, how long it takes, and your average heart rate during the ride. Put all this information into one graph on your refrigerator or on your bathroom mirror or anywhere that you will see it often enough to inspire you. Get the idea?"

"Yes, I do," John replied enthusiastically. "That sort of works like a recipe for tiramisu. You get the ingredients, put them together in the right order and you are set in no time. So for generating 50 percent more leads in our company, I would first look for a challenging project timeframe; maybe three months, because that would really be a big stretch. Then I may discuss it with my brother, who doesn't believe that it is possible. Proving my older brother wrong in what he believes about me is really a huge turn-on! For process feedback, I would get my team together, including all the co-workers in the marketing and sales department who are responsible for generating leads. I would set up a weekly meeting with each of us promising to deliver results next time we meet. Whatever I commit to them in public, I get done, if for no other reason than for the guilt I would feel if they followed through and I failed. And we could set up a little system that documents the leads we generate every day. I could put that onto a blackboard in my office with a graph showing me on a daily basis whether we are moving in the right direction. Is that what you mean by creating a project environment that activates your individual motivators?"

"That is exactly what I mean," the Master replied, "and the beauty of that concept is that as soon as you know what really motivates and inspires you strongly, you become aware of the motivators of your team members and understand that theirs will be different from yours. Think about sales teams. Isn't it sad that a whole industry had motivated their teams for over fifty years with 'competition' as the one and only motivator they know to use effectively? They announce competitions with wonderful prizes like winning a week for two in Hawaii. They spend tons of money on those prizes and then they wonder why only 20 percent of their employees perform better when competing. But the other 80 percent may be motivated by working in teams, or maybe they need action or perhaps a model of excellence. Isn't it a shame that the same 20 percent always win and the same 80 percent always get frustrated because their bosses don't know how to motivate them? Remember, there are fourteen different motivators, as discovered by the Russians, and sales managers usually miss out on thirteen of them!"

"So the hallmark of a good manager is to offer a team environment where all fourteen motivators are offered, so that everybody can find those that support his or her motivation best and get their hearts involved?" John asked, not believing what he was hearing.

"That's correct. Great coaches intuitively offer an environment that gives everybody a chance to get their heart involved. Here is a checklist on how to do that."

Being in action

- People with this motivator need momentum. The more they have to do, the more they get done.
- They need truckloads of work, and
- Tight schedules.

Inspiring examples

- Team members with this motivator need models of excellence.
- Provide case studies from other team members who have already achieved the goals.
- All kinds of inspiring role models—in movies, biographies, success stories from the company's history—are helpful.

Memories

- Provide success journals.
- Discuss successes from the past before you introduce future plans.
- Remind team members of past successes.

Future perspectives

- Provide a career plan.
- Discuss future rewards and career steps in detail.
- Use written "career guarantees" as you would money and stock options.

Making sense/identification

- Take time to explain the reason behind projects.

- Point out the advantages of doing a project in detail.
- Explain the values behind objectives.

Feeling good during performance

- Make sure that personality type and job profile are a good match.
- Allow as much time for preparation as possible.
- Encourage stress-sensitive team members to master self-regulation skills like autogenic training.

Competition

- Set up competitions and rewards.
- Offer different criteria to measure success.
- Competing with friends and colleagues is a lot more fun than anonymous competitions.

Working alone

- Define areas where team members with this motivator have a leadership function.
- Reward them with responsibility.
- Give them resources that create space to realize projects in their own way.

Companionship

- Support team-building.
- Allow for team communication.
- Reward team spirit.

Environment

- Be aware that some team members' motivation is strongly influenced by their surroundings.
- Use furniture, computer, and other tool upgrades as rewards.
- Be sensitive with the needs of team members for decorating their space.

Recognition

- Look for good performances and praise regularly.
- Create rewards (trophies, certificates, etc.).
- Compliment team members in front of others (be credible by offering specific feedback).

Process feedback

- Create feedback loops that show the progress of a project early.
- Allow for easy and regular progress evaluations.
- Create diagrams, graphs, and other feedback tools to document developments over time.

Challenge

- Support team members who need challenges by giving them bigger projects and more responsibility than they have handled in the past.
- Give them goals that really stretch them.
- Tell them honestly (without being strategic) when you have doubts whether they can execute a project.

Preparation

- If possible, allow for preparation time with team members who need it.
- Match projects that need a lot of improvising with team members who thrive on that.
- Allow for preparation time in decision-making processes with team members who need it.

Handing the checklist over to John, the Marketing Master added, "Most managers and entrepreneurs are good at motivating team members who have the same motivators that they do. The challenge is to be flexible enough to create project environments where people have the chance to thrive on their own individual motivators.

"Working with your motivators and systematically creating an environment where people are inspired and motivated in a way that fits their personal preferences best is the hallmark of all great coaches. This is true in sports as well as in business. The more you know yourself, the better you will be able to inspire others. One of your motivators, for example, is challenge. If someone tells you, 'John, you can't do it,' that pushes your button. But the interesting thing is that seven or eight people out of ten sharing their doubts with you only bothers you a little. But two of the ten, maybe your dad or a coach whom you highly respect, would make your motivator kick in full blast.

"One of the most successful entrepreneurs I know in Germany is the youngest of five brothers. When he finished high school, his dad advised him to work for the government, because he suggested he wouldn't have the talent to succeed as an entrepreneur. The dad suggested that this youngest son should leave entrepreneurship to his more talented older brothers.

"The entrepreneur, who has been a client of mine for years, told me, 'That was the last kick I needed. I didn't even go to college and I started my first company with no money when I was nineteen. I wasn't even thirty when I made my first million, and by the time I was thirty-five, my company grossed more profit than all of my brothers' businesses together. My dad died ten years ago, but it doesn't matter. I'm still driven to prove how wrong he was!'"

The Marketing Master looked at John with a smile and a twinkle in his eye and said, "Radiating eyes are not only a magnet to attract customers, they are without question a magnet for entrepreneurs to attract the right team members. I think you deserve an afternoon off on the lake. See you tomorrow at 10:00 AM."

John spent his afternoon in a lounge chair on his hotel's terrace, enjoying the sunshine and daydreaming about his new company. His thoughts were running wild, and finally—after two Bavarian beers to calm down—he wrote in his journal:

- Taking care of my employee's heart: Making sure that everyone of them knows their key motivators.
- Discuss the key motivators with each of them and find out how we can involve them in the projects every team member is managing.
- Have a team meeting where every member reports his or her motivators, so that the whole group develops an understanding of what is most inspiring and motivating to each of them.
- Invite the whole group to discuss the fourteen motivators and make suggestions how we as a company can activate each one of them to motivate the whole team!

Chapter 8: The Seventh Heart Magnet: Attracting clients with the right talents to the right positions

"Congratulations, John!" The Marketing Master greeted John with his infectious smile and invited him in for the last session. "Today we'll put the most important key into place when it comes to realizing your marketing plan. I have pondered for years why some of my clients grasp these concepts rapidly while others take months or years and may still only assimilate half of it.

"After much analysis, I discovered that the bottleneck was neither marketing skills nor motivation, it was simply a **lack of talent**. To phrase it differently, they were missing the right person in the right place.

"Due to excellent marketing and management research during the last years, there is now scientific evidence specifying why marketing concepts often don't work.

"The Gallup Institute did a study, interviewing more than 1.7 million employees from over a hundred companies in thirty-nine countries. One of their questions was: **'Do you have the opportunity to use your greatest talents and strengths on a daily basis in your job?'**

"Only one out of five employees agreed with that statement! A whopping 80 percent of the employees answered that they couldn't use their greatest strengths. The implication is that GE or Siemens or any other industry giant with 100,000 employees does not fully use the potential of 80,000 of their team members. What's worse is that research shows again and again that when people aren't given the opportunity to display their strengths, they are less confident, motivated, enduring, and less willing to be perseverant. Most importantly, from a marketing point of view, **they are not able to perform at the level of their peers who are using their talent and who attract clients easily.** That's the reason Jim Collins, one of my favorite management coaches, points out that in the long run, the restricting growth factor of a company is its ability to attract the people with the right strengths to get the job done.

"Lack of talented people is a huge handicap, especially for small and medium-sized companies. If your marketing department consists of one or two people, or if your sales team is less than a handful and those people don't have the right talent for the job, your customers and your company suffer severely.

"Let me give you an example: Years ago, I worked for a leading consulting company in Switzerland. In their niche, they were the world market leader for a software company that controlled production processes. I was invited to prepare their salespeople for a convention in Saudi Arabia. What they called their 'sales team' consisted of the most introverted and shy group of computer programmers I had ever met. During class, some of them confessed that they had often chosen night jobs in an attempt to avoid contact with other employees. Transforming this group of engineers and programmers into strong contact-building sales representatives would take an act of God, and a lot more time than I had! I informed their boss that I would need at least one strong *contactor*, someone with the talent to connect with people.

"When I asked for their most talented *people person,* I noticed numerous grins from the group. They agreed unanimously that it was the Italian chauffeur who spent his days driving the car for the boss. It took me some time to convince the owner to allow his chauffeur to fly over to represent his company at the sales convention in Saudi Arabia, but I can be quite convincing.

"When they returned home, they had three times more leads than from the last three sales events. One of the programmers described the scenario with enthusiasm, saying, 'This guy from Italy was incredible! Whenever a visitor looked in the direction of our booth, he made eye contact, smiled and invited him to have an original latte macchiato from Italy. He didn't know anything about our products, but he knew everything about making people feel good with small talk. He was the catalyst to our success.'"

The Master looked at John and said, "The famous Peter Drucker pointed out that there are only two true functions in any company, marketing and innovation; everything else is cost.

"If that's true, ***it is the obligation of any entrepreneur is to make sure that at least the key functions of his company, marketing and innovation, are in the hands of talented people who are qualified to get the job done.***

"Here are some important questions for entrepreneurs who want to implement the Concept of the Seven Magnets and make it work for their companies:

1. What are my greatest talents and strengths that I should focus on as an entrepreneur?
2. What are my main weaknesses that I need to compensate for with a team that has complementary strengths?
3. Are my key players in sales and marketing talented and placed in positions to do the best possible job?
4. If not, do I look at talent-hunting as one of my most important jobs—do I take it as seriously as any talent scout in Major League Baseball does?"

John moved forward and said, "Stop for a minute. That's a huge concept. Give me a minute to digest it. If I understand you correctly, what you are saying is that a lot of marketing and sales concepts are not put into practice as effectively as they could be. One of the main reasons is that entrepreneurs don't look at marketing as one of the two key factors of their company. They don't perceive the need to find and hire the best talents as a priority; therefore they don't see themselves as talent scouts. Because they accept average talents, they get average results at best."

"That's exactly what I mean," the Marketing Master agreed, "but I will go a step further. I urge the entrepreneur to become very clear about his own talents. Take any kind of management book you choose. What they all teach is the myth of the well-rounded entrepreneur and manager who knows it all and does it all when it comes to leadership and management. It is simply a myth. The last human being thought to be talented enough to know it all was Leonardo da Vinci. Since then, most great entrepreneurs have mastered only two or three fields of entrepreneurship effectively. **Part of the secret of the most successful entrepreneurs has been in recognizing their limits and finding talented team members to compensate for their weaknesses. That is the key that makes the difference!"**

"How do you teach your clients to figure out where they are great and where to hire talents to build teams with complementary strengths?" John wanted to know.

"There is another big study from the Gallup Institute, where they interviewed 2.3 million managers and compared the answers of the 3 percent who achieved top results with their average peers.

"The average manager believed that:

- Nearly anybody can learn to become competent in everything—it is only a question of training, and
- The biggest potential for growth is where people have weaknesses.

"The managers who achieved the top results gave very different answers. They believed that:

- There is little value in training people to work on their weaknesses. They won't change much, and being average in something is still not attractive to customers.
- There is great value in unfolding people's strengths. When people discover their greatest talents, they are motivated, learn fast, and deliver great results.

"With that in mind, I would like to teach our clients how they can find their greatest strengths quickly and easily and learn how to focus on them. Would you like to test this method for yourself?"

John nodded with excitement. "Is it any kind of personality test like the MMPI or the MBTI?"

"Actually, it is even easier than that. We worked with a lot of personality tests and discovered the ones that deliver the most accurate results when it comes to measuring attitudes or behavior.

"But when it comes to figuring out your strengths, there is nothing better than an analysis of your personal history and your individual preferences. Our talents build such strong patterns that you can detect them everywhere. But as a Chinese proverb teaches, "The last thing on earth a fish will discover is water." We often have a hard time recognizing the obvious."

The Master paused and invited John to participate in an exercise.

Analyzing your personal history for talents and strengths

- Recall as many emotional highlights from your childhood as you can.
- Think about the emotional highlights when you were active. Which activities made your heart sing?
- What were the activities occurring when you forgot everything else around you?
- According to your parents, grandparents, siblings, and friends, what are the things you are most enthusiastic about?
- Finally, the grandmother test. (If she is still alive, ask her!) If somebody had asked your grandmother when you were ten years old what kind of kid you were, what would she have answered?

Analyzing your activity preferences in the present

- Analyze your daily routine for fourteen days. Which activities are you drawn to and which do you avoid?
- What is easiest for you?
- What do you enjoy most?

- Which activities give you energy and wings to fly?
- Which activities drag you down?
- Where are you a fast learner?
- What subjects are you so interested in learning that you find your memory is better than usual?
- The enthusiasm indicator: About which activities in my life are you the most enthusiastic?
- What are you looking forward to the most?

"When you think of a single talent as a single note in music, then the combination of talents creates the melody we play in life. Looking at very successful entrepreneurs, we very often find that some patterns and combinations of talents show up repeatedly.

"One very insightful study was done by Roger Hamilton. Analyzing some of the greatest entrepreneurs and marketing geniuses, he found that eight different talent combinations surface repeatedly. I use his categories and examples to help my clients discover the direction of their greatest strengths. Do you want to do a simple test to find the easiest path to your breakthrough success?"

With enthusiasm, John clapped his hands in anticipation of the next step. "Let's go for it! This is exactly why I'm here."

"The first talent combination is the *Star*: People like Lee Iacocca, Arnold Schwarzenegger, or Martha Stewart fall into this category. These people are very much driven to brand themselves and become well known in their industry.

"The next talent combination is the *Creator*: People like Bill Gates or X and Y, and the founders of Google fall into this category. They visualize companies, systems, and new technologies that did not exist before and create new industries.

"The third talent combination is the *Mechanic*: People like Sam Walton or Michael Dell fall into this category of great system engineers. These entrepreneurs are really good at building systems and outperforming their competitors in their field for years or even decades.

"The fourth category Hamilton calls *Lord*. People like Andrew Carnegie, John D. Rockefeller, and others who built empires through the leadership of their strong and often patriarchal personalities belong into this group.

"The fifth category is the *Accumulator*. People like Warren Buffett or Sir John Templeton fall into this category: Their primary talent is collecting, accumulating stocks, money, information, or whatever their area of expertise is until they reach a critical mass.

"The sixth category is the *Trader*. George Soros and Nelson Bunker Hunt are examples for the talent of creating a fortune by playing the stock market their way … and yes, sometimes they lose big too.

"The seventh talent combination to major success is the *Deal Maker*. Donald Trump and private-equity guru Stephen Schwarzman belong to that category.

"The eighth talent combination Roger Hamilton discovered is the *Supporter*. People like Steve Ballmer or Colin Powell fall into this category. They combine a very strong personality with the desire to support others who are even more in the spotlight."

The Marketing Master smiled and asked, "Is there any type and category that resonates strongly with you?"

John nodded. "I am most definitely a creator. I'm always coming up with inspiring ideas and concepts. I can re-invent my business every day if I have to. I even re-invent things when there is no need to, just for the fun of doing it. The problem is that after I have invented an idea, I start losing interest. I'm great at starting, I can motivate and inspire people with my ideas, but I'm not a good finisher."

"That is exactly the insight I was hoping you would grasp. There is no need to be good at everything; you can't be. If you want your company and your marketing to succeed, you must learn to manage your weaknesses. In your case, as a creator, you need members with the qualities of a Steve Ballmer to support you, or somebody like mechanics and system engineer Michael Dell whose talent and pride it is to take your idea and build the perfect system around it.

“Let me give you a hypothetical scenario:

“You bought your company for $50 million. Your goal is to double your investment in five years. Analyzing your management team from an outside perspective, as an investor who cares for the long-term growth and value of the company, which of the members of your management team would you keep in order to achieve your goal, and which ones would you replace with new members who were more talented and better able to support your creative CEO?”

“Whoa, that is really hard to answer! We are a management team of three. One of my partners is my brother-in-law. He is so average that I even don’t know where he could be hiding a special talent. The other is one of my best friends. He is really brilliant and has at least as many killer ideas as I do. I really love discussing new concepts with him.”

“So, what is your prognosis of doubling your company’s value during the next five years with that team?”

“Do you want an honest answer?” John exhaled slowly.

“Would I serve you as a coach if I would accept less than that?”

John shook his head. “Well, the honest answer is I should fire my brother-in-law first thing when I come home and replace his job with a good systems engineer.”

“What about your good friend? Is he an asset to achieve the goals you set?”

“I love discussing ideas with him, but honestly, we always inspire each other to come up with even crazier ideas.”

“Does that help to get things done?”

“No, it doesn’t. But when I think about the neighbor with whom I play tennis, he is a great systems developer. But he is the bore of every party.”

"That's exactly why a lot of average entrepreneurs surround themselves with people with talents similar to their own. That may help the chemistry, but it slows down the process of achieving results. You need to set your priorities straight. If your comfort zone at work is more important than reaching your goals, it's fine to surround yourself with people who are like you. But if you want to achieve results, it's imperative that you grow as a person. Only when you can build great relationships with people who are very different from you can you build a powerful team with all the talents needed for your success. Your similarities will be in your values, but not necessarily in your thinking style or your talents, on the contrary."

There was a long pause and John was deep in thought, thinking through what the Marketing Master had just told him. Finally he said: "Wow that is powerful! You really widened my mental map about what is necessary to be successful as an entrepreneur. The more I think about it, the clearer it becomes that the best marketing plan is only as good as it is executed. Even if every individual in your team has great talents, but together their strengths don't encompass those needed to make it to the top, the best marketing concept can't and won't compensate for it."

The Marketing Master beamed. "It took me more than ten years to become consistent in my coaching successes. As long as I was improving the marketing strategy or tactics when things didn't work out, I was looking in the wrong ballpark. Only when I started matching the talents of the people with the demands of the marketing plan, success became consistent. And consistency is the hallmark of all champions."

John looked the Marketing Master directly in the eyes. "I've got twelve hours on my flight back from Munich to Los Angeles to figure out the solution of how to let my brother-in-law go and find a new job for my good friend and co-creator. Then I need to find the right supporters and mechanics for all my creative ideas to help build the company."

"That's the way to do it," the Marketing Master agreed. "Why don't you join my wife and me for dinner tonight? Let's have some fun in the Bavarian Alps before you fly home. You can't leave without enjoying some German beer!"

BUY A SHARE OF THE FUTURE IN YOUR COMMUNITY

These certificates make great holiday, graduation and birthday gifts that can be personalized with the recipient's name. The cost of one S.H.A.R.E. or one square foot is $54.17. The personalized certificate is suitable for framing and will state the number of shares purchased and the amount of each share, as well as the recipient's name. The home that you participate in "building" will last for many years and will continue to grow in value.

Here is a sample SHARE certificate:

THIS CERTIFIES THAT

YOUR NAME HERE

HAS INVESTED IN A HOME FOR A DESERVING FAMILY

1985-2005

TWENTY YEARS OF BUILDING FUTURES IN OUR COMMUNITY ONE HOME AT A TIME

1200 SQUARE FOOT HOUSE @ $65,000 = $54.17 PER SQUARE FOOT

This certificate represents a tax deductible donation. It has no cash value.

YES, I WOULD LIKE TO HELP!

I support the work that Habitat for Humanity does and I want to be part of the excitement! As a donor, I will receive periodic updates on your construction activities but, more importantly, I know my gift will help a family in our community realize the dream of homeownership. ***I would like to SHARE in your efforts against substandard housing in my community!*** *(Please print below)*

PLEASE SEND ME ___________ SHARES at $54.17 EACH = $ $____________

In Honor Of: ____

Occasion: *(Circle One)* *HOLIDAY* *BIRTHDAY* *ANNIVERSARY*

OTHER: ____

Address of Recipient: ____

Gift From: _______________ ***Donor Address:*** ______________________________

Donor Email: ____

I AM ENCLOSING A CHECK FOR $ $_____________ PAYABLE TO HABITAT FOR HUMANITY <u>OR</u> PLEASE CHARGE MY VISA OR MASTERCARD *(CIRCLE ONE)*

Card Number ___________________________________ Expiration Date: ____________

Name as it appears on Credit Card __________________ Charge Amount $ ____________

Signature ____

Billing Address ____

Telephone # Day ___________________________ Eve ___________________________

PLEASE NOTE: Your contribution is tax-deductible to the fullest extent allowed by law.

Habitat for Humanity • P.O. Box 1443 • Newport News, VA 23601 • 757-596-5553

www.HelpHabitatforHumanity.org